Sauce
On
Sunday

*An Ancestral Journey to Find My
Sicilian Roots*

Janet Sierzant

Sauce on Sunday
Copyright© Revision 2022 Janet Sierzant
ISBN: 978-1-970153-01-9
Library of Congress Control Number: 2018914339

All rights reserved. No part of this book may be reproduced, stored in a retrieval system, or transmitted in any form or by any means without the author's prior written permission except by a reviewer who may quote brief passages in a review printed in a newspaper, magazine, or journal.

Maps
Google maps
Planet Ware
Lonely Planet

La Maison Publishing
Vero Beach, Florida
The Hibiscus City
www.lamaisonpublishing.com

Map of Sicily from Lonely Planet

While sitting at a restaurant with two of my fellow authors, one asked me about my Sicilian background. I laughed and said, "All I know is we always have sauce on Sunday." My friends joined in the laughter, but I soon realized I didn't know too much about the maternal part of my heritage. Once I left the confines of Little Italy and the Italian neighborhoods of New York, words like *mutzadell* for mozzarella, *ree-goth* for ricotta, and *gabaladina* for eggplant didn't have the same meaning. I learned to speak the language of *Metagon or American,* adapting to my environment and thus losing yet another aspect of my culture. I've been to Italy before, but never made it to Sicily. I only knew the name of the small fishing village, Sciacca, pronounced ("shock-a,") located on Sicily's southern coast, where my grandfather, Giuseppe Corrao, grew up.

The writer's side of my brain started churning. Sauce on Sunday! What an excellent title for a book.

Now, any authentic Italian in New York knows the rich tomato blend simmering on the stove as *gravy.* Gravy on Sunday? No! I don't think the title has the same zing.

Dedicated to my grandfather
Giuseppe Corrao

1895-1968

My grandfather always looked old, maybe because I never saw any pictures of him when he was younger. His cane leaned up against the wall next to his bed. He used it to get to his recliner or the small bathroom in the hall. Giuseppe spent much of his time at the park with Sicilian friends. When he was home, he sat in front of a television, watching wrestling matches.

At the time, I was only sixteen and had no interest in family history. My grandfather rarely spoke to me because he preferred to speak in Italian. So many years later, I realized he had a story to tell.

Although my mother had suffered a stroke that wiped out many of her recollections, I managed to get a basic family tree. She did recall some stories of her relatives, but only enough to make me more curious. I signed up for a free week's trial on one of the popular ancestry sites. Still, I found nothing to bridge the way back to Italy. Then, I discovered the Genealogy Society at my local library. There, I met a woman experienced in digging up the roots of her family. Her name was Adeline, and she offered to help me. We located my grandfather's birth certificate and discovered my great-grandparents' names, Paolo Corrao and Maria Colletti. Maybe my great-grandparents had brothers and sisters back in Italy.

The curiosity about my ancestry gnawed at me. Maybe it was time to take a trip to Italy.

La Famiglia Giuseppe Corrao and Anna

Table of Contents

Back to the Beginning 1
Meow Mix 6
Cork Screwed 8

Trip 1

Pit Stop in Palermo 11
Supermarcato 15
Homeless in Palermo 19
The Road to Sciacca 23
The Lay of the Land 29
Piazza 32
Three Levels 37
Old Italian Men 39
Migration 43
Portas 47
Dolce Vita 50
Sauce or Gravy 53
Holiday 59
Remnants of the Past 63
The Harbor 67
The Boat Yard 71
Spiaggia 74

Pistachio Cream 77
What's in a Name 79
Monte San Calogero 82
Close Encounter 87
Feline Persuasion 92
Reunion 96

Trip 2
Dumped in Milan 98
Lost Baggage 102
Amore 108
Bocce Ball 113
Dirty Bird 117
Pani e Panelle 120
Family Homestead 123
Rock of Regina 128
Cimitero 133
Corrao Fratelli 136
Pizza Mia 139
Armenian Detour 141
Bellevue del Golfo 144
The Last Corrao Daughter 146

Trip 3

Palermo 151

Nine Digits 155

Marzipan Lambs 157

Marsala 159

Crypts and Stones 165

Buona Pasqua 169

Flavors of Sciacca 172

Famiglia Per Sempre 175

The Grotto 179

San Biagio 182

My Heart is in Sciacca 184

The Crypt Keeper 188

Cugini 195

Castello Luna 201

Recca 207

Cefalù 210

Saturday Market 213

Hairy Situation 215

Trip 4

Sicilian Artisans 218

Sea Glass 222

Termi di Sciacca 226

Italian Wedding 230
Good Medicine 233
Full Circle 240
Recipes 247
    Jeanette Corrao's Sunday Gravy 249
    Ricotta Pie 250
    Coponata 251
    Pistachio Cream 252
    Creamy Salmon and Pasta 253
    Eggplant and Sausage 254
    Seafood Paella 255
    Artichoke Hearts 256
    Pasticcotti Pockets 257
    Zucchini Pesto 258
    Sausage with Lemon and Oregano 259
    Pistachio Pesto 260
    Stuffed Squid in Tomato Sauce 261
    Anisette Cookies 262
    Giusy's Potato Pie 263

Back to the Beginning

In my thirties, the urge to travel came on in full force. I'd take off to Europe at the drop of a suggestion. The world opened to me, and I didn't think it would end until I found myself divorced and on a tight budget. The sound of a jet overhead made me melancholy as I imagined where it was going, without me!

"You can't go to Italy by yourself," some said. "You can't afford to spend your money on such frivolity," others insisted. "You may need your money for health care in your old age."

Well, that did it! I was more determined than ever. I threw their cautions to the wind and put my journey to the "motherland" into motion.

Traveling alone would make most women nervous, and I'm no exception. I recognized the pitfalls and challenges of landing in the middle of a country where I didn't know the language. I took a few deep breaths to relax and decided to go along with whatever presented itself. I found a round-trip flight from JFK Airport to Palermo for only six hundred dollars. Something came over me, and I hit Book It! Then reality set in. Riley jumped up on my desk. *Oh, crap! What will I do with my cat?* Luckily, my daughter agreed to take care of him.

I'd stay in Palermo for one night and then jump onto a bus the next day for Sciacca. There, I would climb the Sicilian hillsides and smell the Mediterranean Sea.

Small, with an olive complexion, my mother considered herself of true Italian blood. But Italians on the mainland of Italy generally have a negative impression of Sicilians.

Once, Sophia Loren appeared on a talk show and commented that Sicilians weren't real Italians. She never liked Sophia after that, and it weighed heavily on my mind.

The northern district of Italy ate white sauces and meaty entrees. In contrast, their southern neighbors ate more fish and tomato-based sauces, but that by itself didn't account for the silent civil war.

Even though my mother knew a few phrases in Italian, they were mostly about food. She understood the language when she was very young. After her mother died, the memory of the Italian language began to fade. It saddened me that such a rich culture had withered. I'd have to sift through the remnants of my mother's broken memories. She was excited when I told her of my plans to visit Sciacca. I relived the happiness on her face every time I mentioned it because the beginnings of dementia had ravaged her short-term memory. Ever since she had a stroke, she hasn't been well. If she dies, the loss will affect me significantly. I don't know how I'll grieve. I'm sure the reality will slap me in the face, and it scares me. There was so much that I didn't know about my mother. I asked questions about her family, but she wasn't much help.

My friend, Celia, from the Italian club, suggested looking up my grandfather's surname in the Italian White Pages. This way, I could write letters before my trip, inquiring whether anyone was related to me. She also suggested I write to the Comune, or city hall, in Sciacca and let them know I was coming. With this in mind, I wrote a letter explaining that I wanted to track my ancestors and told them I didn't speak Italian.

I found five Corrao families and then wrote each of them a note in English and translated it into Italian on Google Translate. I included my grandfather's birth certificate and the link to my Facebook page, just in case they were online.

I planned to stay at an Airbnb when I arrived in Palermo. It was my first time using the service, and I wasn't sure if I'd like it. It was a privately owned studio apartment, so I'd be alone, unlike a hotel or traditional bed and breakfast, where other guests often interact. In a few short months, I'd make my way to Sciacca.

Lured by the patio that overlooked the city, I took a chance and booked it. My host, Toni, sent me directions to her apartment from the airport and promised to meet me there with the key. She was expecting a baby, but promised to help me find the bus to Sciacca the next day. I've heard Italian people are known for their hospitality, something I'd be relying on once I arrive.

Committed to my expedition, I searched for Italian courses online. Learning a new language was difficult. Everything drained from my brain within hours. Then, I had the brilliant idea of downloading a translation app on my smartphone.

Wait! *What if my phone dies, or if I need an internet connection?* The small village where I'd be staying was not a tourist area. I pictured myself in the middle of Sciacca, trying to communicate with my hands. *That's how most Italians express themselves anyway.* The thought made me laugh.

Hmm. I would have to learn a little *questo* and *quella*, "This" and "that" in Italian. Sicilian Italian is entirely different from basic Italian. If that were the case, I'd be back to waving my hands around like an overenthusiastic mime.

Six weeks went by, and I had almost forgotten about connecting with my ancestral relatives when, one day, a strange man from Sicily sent me a Facebook request. His name was Vincenzo. *Hmm*, I thought, *not bad looking*. Maybe when I get to Italy, I'll have an *Eat, Pray, Love* moment. I'm definitely up for eating, but the love part was a little scary.

Shortly after, I received another response. "Hi Janet, my husband's grandmother, Caterina Corrao, just received your letter concerning your family history research. One of Caterina's sons plans to go to the city hall of Sciacca to get some information. I will let you know as soon as possible. Josie."

Josie was originally from Boston. She was younger than I was. We didn't have much in common, except that she spoke English. We became friends on Facebook, and I told her of my plans to come in the spring. I already had a place to stay in Palermo but needed to find a room in Sciacca. She suggested a B&B called Fazio's. I booked it and told her I'd be coming from Palermo on the bus. Josie offered to pick me up even though she was five months pregnant. *Geez! Is everyone in Italy having a baby?*

Since I tend to isolate myself, I was determined to get out of the B&B as much as possible. My friend Lorrie insisted that I find out how Sicilians make their sauce, primarily because of the title of my book. So, I found some local cooking classes, but they were expensive. Perhaps Josie would invite me over, and I could ask how she makes hers.

Realizing that I didn't know what was going on in the world, I forced myself to catch up on the day's current events. Airstrikes ordered by U.S. forces in Syria were troubling, along with talk of a preemptive strike on North Korea due to nuclear testing. The mounting crisis loomed on the world stage, and I was about to put myself out there. It seemed like Americans always had to be on the defensive. My own opinions about politics didn't matter, but I wondered how the people of Sicily felt about it. After all, they had been invaded by many countries in the past.

Most Italians living in Italy had preconceived ideas of America based on what they had heard on the news. I felt the same fear when I left my home in New York to live in Georgia. Fear of the KKK and Southern bias toward Yankees had me in a state of anxiety. Although I appreciated the lush green foliage, I missed Long Island, the smell of the ocean, the salty air, and the churning waves along a sandy beach.

Living in Georgia, I felt homesick. Although I missed Long Island, going back to live there was out of the question. Sometimes, you can't go back to the place where you belong. Maybe it was the same for Italian immigrants. Some returned to their homeland, but most stayed because they started a new life, married, and had new families.

Meow Mix

The night before my trip to Sicily, I lay in bed and stared out the open blinds of the window. Watching the full moon move across the night sky, I realized I wouldn't see the sunrise in the morning. I felt a little melancholy about leaving my comfortable life to travel across the world. I'd have to give up the familiar for the unknown. Maybe I'd appreciate my life all the more once I returned. That's usually the case, like when the electricity goes out, and you have no power. Once it turns on again, you realize the value you'd taken for granted—for a while, anyway.

As soon as I dozed off, my cell phone chimed. *Geez! I was afraid of that!* Usually, I left the phone in the living room, but I set it next to my bed since it was the only alarm clock I had.

Now, I was wide awake, anticipating another text.

I woke up to the cellphone alarm. Over the years, my cat Riley has served as my wake-up call. He'd start by gently clawing the covers, and when that didn't work, he'd bite my cheek. I had to keep the pillow over my head, but I sensed him staring expectantly, hoping I'd wake up to feed him.

Animals supposedly have no concept of time or awareness of separation, but Riley seemed to sense I was going somewhere without him. From the moment I pulled out a suitcase, he decided to sleep in it.

In protest, he stopped using the litter box. Concerned, I tried everything on the market to help him—hairball remedy, canned pumpkin, and even olive oil. After one week, I had to take him to the vet.

Dr. Stein fixed him up and told me to feed him Meow Mix.

"Meow Mix?" I said.

"Yeah! Cats ask for it by name."

He's a funny guy.

I followed his prescription, but was back in his office five days later.

"Look, he's an old cat," Dr. Stein said. "This is common. That's just the way it is."

My eyes filled with tears. "What are you saying, doctor?"

"I'm saying that you may have to make a hard decision soon."

My daughter agreed to stay over and take care of Riley while I was gone. I bought him some Meow Mix, Ping-Pong balls, and a few catnip toys to occupy him. Although I arranged for his comfort, I didn't want him to feel lonely. He'd probably need a kitty shrink by the time I returned.

Riley wasn't like most cats; he had no travel anxiety. Usually, I took him with me wherever I went. I'd strap him in the backseat in his carrier, and he'd curl up and go to sleep. I gave him extra wet food in his bowl to ease my guilt. He looked at me with crazy eyes, as if expecting something to happen, and then took a lick of the food. Not hungry, he followed me into the bathroom to watch me put on my makeup. I kissed him goodbye and told him not to die, recalling Dr. Stein's warning. He had me a little worried.

Cork Screwed

Expecting it to take an eternity to get through JFK airport screening, I was pleasantly surprised when the attendant handed me a pre-check pass. At least someone remembered how much I had traveled previously, although it didn't do me much good. My suitcase came under suspicion as it moved on the conveyor belt. The TSA agent pulled it aside, and I had to remove my shoes and walk through the screening machine again. I longed for the days when the passengers didn't have to stand in line in their stocking feet. It's amazing. All it took was one nut job with a shoe bomb to change the lives of every weary traveler. Anyway, I followed my suitcase and gave them permission to rummage. I tried to shed light on the item in question as things started flying out. The screener pointed to an image. It seemed to be in my toiletry case. *Surely, they're not banning tweezers now, are they?* When I moved to lift the case from my luggage, the attendant threw his arm out to block me.

"You're not allowed to touch the bag."

He emptied the contents and lifted the corkscrew.

"This item is not allowed on the plane," he lectured. "I'll have to confiscate it."

I laughed. "Really?"

"Really!"

He stood back and let me jam my belongings back into the suitcase. Of course, it wasn't as neat and meticulous as when I first packed, and the contents seemed to take up more room than before. It's funny how that happens.

"Here, I'll help you," he said and crushed down the cover with one hand while he zipped it up with the other.

He must have seen my annoyance just under the surface because he offered to give me an envelope so I could mail the corkscrew back to myself.

"No, thanks!" I said. "It's just a corkscrew."

He might have had a point—it could be a weapon. If anyone messed with me, I might have used it to poke their eye out.

A crying baby caught my attention as I waited to board the plane to Italy.

"Anyone with children can board first," they announced.

I love babies as much as the next guy, but why do they get special treatment for inconveniencing everyone else? Why don't they have a family flight, where all the babies and parents could fly in shared misery? I thought.

The other passengers and I slowly inched down the jet bridge. A uniformed agent scanned each boarding pass. As I approached, she eyed my suitcase.

"I'm going to have to weigh that before you can board with it," she said, lifting it onto a scale. "I'm sorry. This case is one kilo more than we allow for a carry-on. I'm going to have to check it. You can retrieve your bag at baggage claim when you land in Sicily." She tore off a ticket and handed it to me. When we reached the plane's entrance, the steward directed everyone to his left. She glanced at my ticket and pointed to her right. Much to my joy, there weren't many passengers in my section. *Was I in First Class?* I held my breath until we backed out of the terminal, then sighed with relief. I had my eye on the five empty seats in the middle aisle, just waiting for me to lift the armrests and claim my bed for the night. *Hmm— maybe my luck was changing.*

The flight attendants came around with beverages, snacks, wine, and more snacks. After dinner, they dimmed the lights, which was the last time we saw them. Because it was a discount airline, if you wanted anything, including water, you had to go to the back of the plane, where they set up a meager array of refreshments. I didn't have the stamina, so I closed my eyes and listened to the distant wailing from the end of the aircraft—the same "special" child who had been having a tantrum in the terminal. As she screeched and howled, I felt bad for the passengers around her. Just as I was falling into an anticipated slumber, someone poked me. It was the stewardess requesting that I go back to my seat. She told me it wasn't fair to the rest of the passengers. I obeyed and went back to my assigned place. The stewardess lowered the serving trays as a stance to keep the seats off limits. Once she was gone, other passengers began sleeping across empty seats. In defiance, I went back, only now I had a hard time going back to sleep. The child in the back was having a meltdown, and the sound penetrated deep into my brain. I felt terrible for the parents, who had no control over the situation. At the same time, the Nazi stewardess came back to evict me.

"Sorry," she said, "you must return to your seat."

This time, someone else jumped into the empty places once she was gone, but she never returned. I dug out my eye mask and tried to curl up on two seats. Suddenly, the cries from the child in the back grew louder. I lifted my weary head to see her and her mother being escorted to the seat behind me! The baby cried for most of the flight.

La Cala - Palermo

Pit Stop in Palermo

After a nine-hour flight and less than two hours of sleep, dehydrated from the dry cabin air, I felt like roadkill. I stumbled off the plane and went through a passport check, then followed the crowd to retrieve my luggage, praying they hadn't lost it. If they could lose Anthony Bourdain's baggage, it could surely happen to me. The hideous red case I bought at Goodwill beckoned from ten feet away. At the time, I thought it was a steal at twelve dollars, only to find a broken zipper on the front pocket. But it had a working handle and wheels, something my old standby did not, so I dragged it behind me to ground transportation.

Toni, the Airbnb host where I was staying, had asked me to text her when I was en route. I switched the phone off airplane mode and waited for a signal, but my phone said no service. *What? No service?* I intended to take a bus, but couldn't access the Google translator without my phone. I looked outside at a dismal rainy day and thought about it. *Do I want to navigate in a strange city with no way of communicating? Who knew where I'd end up?* A girl on the plane advised me to take a taxi.

"Where's the adventure in that?" I had replied, but now, it seemed like a good idea.

Bombarded by a slew of cabbies, I took the first one. What was I supposed to do? Give them a job interview? He headed out of the airport in stone silence. If he knew any English, he was stingy with it. Fine with me. After struggling with the tiny airline pillow and getting little sleep, I felt a headache coming on. I wasn't in the mood to talk anyway.

Mr. Wonderful dumped me in the heart of Palermo Centre across from the *Palazzo Mirto Museo*. This museum holds one of Italy's most precious collections of the Punic Wars and Ancient Greek art. He pointed to the meter. "Fifty-six euros," he said.

I found out later that the fare shouldn't have cost more than twenty-five euros. Many people back home told me to watch out for pickpockets and swindlers in Italy. It was my lesson on being ripped off in Italy, and I vowed to be more vigilant.

A long, narrow alley stretched before me, Via Orologio. I was looking for the number 21. Dragging my suitcase along the cobblestone surface, I passed construction workers. They looked me up and down and then tried to speak. "Non parlo italiano," I said and continued walking down the alleyway. Unable to find the apartment, I pulled my suitcase back toward the main road. The wheels squeaked in protest as I rolled it over the rough pavement.

Luckily, I found a store on the corner, and the man knew a little English. I asked him to call Toni, the apartment owner, and dialed the number on my phone.

Rambling in Italian, the only word he said that I understood was Janet. He hung up and informed me that my host was on the way.

Toni E. Leonarda finally showed up with the keys. Much to my surprise, *she was a he*. The i at the end of his name threw me off.

"Sorry," he said, "my wife just had the baby, and I got delayed at the hospital."

"I understand," I said. "I'm just relieved to see you."

Toni took my suitcase, and I followed him to the apartment. The number was missing from the entrance. He opened the door, and we entered a hall with marble flooring and stairs with wrought-iron railings. There was no elevator, so we climbed six flights to the very top of the building. I had arrived!

I was thrilled. I put my suitcase in the separate bedroom off the living room, and Toni showed me around the kitchen. Everything was modern, but the oven had me concerned. It was gas, and I was only used to electricity. He showed me how to light it. Thinking I might burn the place down, I decided to avoid the oven and stick with the stovetop. Glass sliding doors led to a balcony with a spectacular view of the city's rooftops.

Toni left. As tired as I was, I danced around the apartment, looking at everything in my temporary home.

Since I had no phone connection and AT&T was still sleeping, I put the nearly dead cell phone on a charger and went to sleep, too. After four hours of rest and a nice hot shower, I felt better and tackled customer service via Internet chat. They were able to tweak some settings, and presto! I had essential communication with the rest of the world. With my battery revived, I took the keys and ventured into a completely new world. Along the way, I ducked into the same small café on the corner to get an extra shot of caffeine.

Sensing a stranger in their midst, some neighbors came out to investigate. Although they spoke broken English, I understood them for the most part. Maybe the language is embedded somewhere in my DNA, a deep-seated knowledge that never disappeared. I communicated with the older folks through their use of sparse English and my translating smartphone. Their curiosity was welcome as they eagerly questioned life in America. They spoke of how their relatives had left Sicily to brave the New World and that they wanted to go there someday. I saw a spark of desire in their eyes.

I was pleasantly surprised that most young people grasped the English language and even used it among themselves. They said that they were required to learn English in school. I recalled my academic beginnings and the French class in sixth grade. Unfortunately, a foreign language wasn't a required class. I didn't go any further until I was in college. During my first year, I signed up for French. My father scolded me and said I should have been studying Italian. I wish that I had listened to him.

Domenica Aperrto

Supermarcato

It amazed me how much Palermo resembled Brooklyn. I see Brooklyn through my memory's eye, warped from how it existed when I was a child. The tiny, neat homes, two to a building, all with unique décor, gave the feeling of conformity. The Good Humor ice-cream trucks came down the street, ringing their bell, as did the carnival rides, like the whip and the half-moon, to thrill the children. Across the street from my house was a park. It was under the El, the subway train that ran above ground. The textile mills were down the block, where local women sat at sewing machines from dawn to dusk, enduring the bite of winter and the heat of summer. It was a tight-knit community. Every component had its place and worked off each other. On the other hand, Brooklyn resembled Palermo since half of the population seemed to come from Sicily.

It had stopped raining, so I pulled up Google Maps and headed toward the Supermercato. Along the way, I noticed the clothes that swung gently in the breeze from makeshift lines on balconies. Neighbors chatted across from each other, some only four or five feet away, yet in their little corner of the world.

The grocery store overflowed with shoppers. Unfamiliar smells of raw meat and freshly made cheeses had a unique scent. Right off, I noticed the carts into which they put their food. Small wagons with long handles to pull them. Growing up in New York, I always called food carts "wagons." People in Georgia looked at me as if I had two heads. "They're buggies," they insisted. Where I come from, buggy means crazy, and even though I was sometimes accused of being such, I settled on saying, "shopping carts." It seemed so natural to call them wagons. The problem was, by the time I needed one, I realized they were outside and out of reach. I should have put the items down and ventured to find one, but I was still on US time, and my brain wasn't in gear yet.

I headed toward the checkout with my arms full of pasta and wine. Along the way, I spotted two teenage boys in the candy aisle. One in an oversized hoodie was eyeballing the candy while the other looked around. It was apparent they were shoplifting. I tried not to watch, but it intrigued me. I recalled how my brother and I stole candy from the local IGA back in Brooklyn when we were kids. One day, the shop owner grew suspicious and followed us to our corner hangout, where we divided our loot. He took the candy and threatened to tell our parents, putting an end to our hoodlum days. That was before recording devices. I wondered if there were store cameras in Italy. Tempted to use my cell phone camera, I decided against it. Besides, the groceries in my arms grew heavy, so I tagged onto the back of the checkout line.

I climbed the six floors up to the apartment with my bottle of wine, a package of ravioli, and a jar of prepared tomato sauce that made me wary. I never touched the stuff at home, but the ravioli called me, and I needed something to top them. My mother always bought ravioli from the Silver Star Company in Brooklyn. Their truck would park on our street. They were my favorite, partly because they tasted good and came in sheets. My mother let me help break them apart at the perforated edges when I was a young girl. I loved the way the frozen sheet snapped perfectly. It saddened me when the company stopped producing these delicious little pies filled with ricotta cheese.

Stairs to the Apartment

Homeless in Palermo

The best way to learn about Sicilian culture is to study the people, but Sicilians are hard to read. Unless you are family, they keep a barrier up for foreigners. I decided to make eye contact in the hopes of connecting with people I encountered, but as usual, my shyness and insecurities overcame any attempt to reach out.

While searching for a supermercato the day before, I noticed signs for a street food fest and headed back to that part of town. Tents lined the road that was closed to traffic, so I took a long walk down the cobblestone road.

I sensed that I'd find a body of water in the distance. I was right. Straight ahead of me was La Cala Port of Palermo, one of the city's main marinas. It was late afternoon, so the sun's angle glowed on the water. Dazzled by the clarity of the horizon, I had to cross the traffic to get a better picture.

I had to buy a ticket before sampling the many treats at the street food fest. I always remembered street fests as open market venues, where the scent of sausage and peppers drew you in, and the decadent chocolate pastries knocked you off your diet. Before I left Florida, I attended "The Taste of Vero Food Fest," where the tickets cost forty dollars per person. I wanted to participate, but doubted I'd eat enough food to be worth it. When did things change? I liked it better when you could pick which vendor you wanted, but some merchants didn't think the system was fair. At least the food fest in Palermo wasn't expensive. They offered different levels, from the full menu to desserts or beverages. I settled on a sweet treat. More of a savory eater, usually desserts, didn't move me, but a strange pastry caught my eye. Although it was good, it sure would have been better if stuffed with something creamy.

Sicilian people love their cannolis and pastries. It reminded me of my childhood. My mother and sisters always looked forward to their coffee and cake after dinner. It was the highlight of the meal.

Like me, my father, whose family was from the mainland of Italy, preferred everything plain. Mom always had to set aside a cake with no frosting, especially for him, when she baked, which wasn't often. And why should she when there was an Italian bakery on every corner in New York?

As I ate myself into oblivion, I put my camera away and concentrated on being sure-footed on the bumpy cobblestone street. I didn't even make it one block when I noticed a homeless man set up in front of a store. He was sitting on the pavement with an open umbrella at his side. It provided neither shade nor shelter from the rain, so I assumed it was more privacy. His hair was matted, his face weathered like leather, but rose-colored glasses gave him a splash of pigment. Homelessness isn't unfamiliar to me. I couldn't ignore that a homeless person inhabited almost every corner back home in Vero Beach. Bulldozers tore down trees and green space to make way for gated communities and the shopping strips needed to accommodate them. It seemed like more and more homeless people congregated in public places like the park or the library. Maybe they were a byproduct of city growth. Perhaps as the population grew, it strained the city's resources.

It shouldn't have been strange to see this homeless man in Italy. No city is immune, but I had to get a picture. I casually aimed my camera at the man and pretended to be texting. I felt a little guilty until I got home and discovered he had given me the finger. It shook me up a little. I searched *homelessness in Italy* on my phone and learned that migrants make up fifty-eight percent of people facing homelessness in Italy.

Full and happy, I finished the rest of my wine and organized the day's pictures. I felt tired enough to go to sleep. It didn't take long. I opened my eyes, thinking I had slept through the night. I heated water for a cup of tea and fired up my computer. I soon realized it was only 12:30 a.m. I tried to go back to sleep. Thoughts and memories crashed into each other as I tossed and turned. Usually, Riley purring by my side soothed me to sleep. I missed my soft, furry friend and wondered if he was also having a hard time without me. I named him Riley because he was the color of rye. I also convinced myself that he was Irish. Calm but quick of temper, he surely wasn't Italian.

Attached at the hip, my furry friend didn't just sleep with me at night; he slept on me.

Finally, I cried *uncle* and dug through my bag for the Tylenol PM.

Chiesa di Santa Caterina

The Road to Sciacca

The bells across from my balcony rang at eight o'clock in the morning after a much-appreciated break overnight. Within seconds, I heard the sounds of construction workers as they began their day's work. It was also my cue to get dressed and go to the corner for a cappuccino. The rich scent of ground coffee beans greeted me before I even entered. No one seemed to notice me unless I pulled out my cell phone to use the translation app. Otherwise, I was invisible. And why shouldn't I be? I'm of Italian blood with the classic profile of high cheekbones and olive complexion. The only thing I am missing is a full head of luxurious hair. I want to blame my father's side of the family for that one, but my mother was relatively thin of hair herself, as were many women in her family.

Josie had sent a message through Facebook saying she would pick me up from the bus stop in Sciacca. At least that end of the journey was secure. I sat in front of the museum and waited for the taxi Toni had arranged to take me to the bus station. He worried I wouldn't find the bus station, so he showed up. It was a good thing, too. The taxis were parked on the side of the museum, and I was waiting in front. Toni took my suitcase, as he had the first time we met, and I followed him to the corner where a taxi was already waiting.

Toni told the cab driver where I needed to go, and I kissed him on both cheeks, Italian style. "Stay on the bus until the last stop," he said.

The cabbie delivered me to the vicinity of the bus but pointed me in the wrong direction, and I found myself at the wrong place. I ran around like a chicken with no head, trying to find the right location. When I finally found my bus, I had to leave to buy my ticket, which everyone erroneously told me I could buy on the bus. I ran to the small office and used my phone translator to buy a round-trip ticket to Sciacca.

With five minutes to spare, I made it into my seat, my heart thumping wildly. It took a while to regain my composure, but I relaxed once the bus left the city. It traveled southeast through the mountainous terrain. A narrow, twisting road carved through the hills of southern Sicily. Farms and tightly packed housing communities whizzed by until the fields opened to the town of Campofranco, where I saw a wind farm in the distance. How smart, I thought. Even though Italy was an old-world province, someone had the sense to harvest energy from nature. In awe, as we passed through small towns, I stared out the window, trying to imagine my ancestors walking around the same streets. I sat back and read my book between impressive views of the Mediterranean outside the window.

As the road flattens, a sign comes into view. Benvenuti ad Agrigento. The bus made a few stops when we neared the city, rolled into a small parking lot, and stopped at the *Café Gaudí Paninoteca*.

Hugging the Coast of Sciacca

"Is this Sciacca?" I asked the passengers coming out of the bus, but no one understood what I was saying except one man.

"Back," he said and gestured toward the road we had just traveled.

Panicked, I ran to the front of the bus and repeated the question. Luckily, a lady who knew a little English told me I should have gotten off half an hour ago. To my horror, I missed my stop! The second lesson learned — don't take directions literally. I wondered if Italians purposely misdirected foreigners. Maybe it gave them a good laugh.

The lady explained my situation to the bus driver, and he agreed to take me back to Sciacca, but I had to wait an hour for the bus to travel back to Palermo. It was his lunch break.

I called Josie to tell her my dilemma.

"Stay put," she said. My husband knows the café and will come to get you."

As my anxiety calmed down, I bought a cappuccino and sat with the bus driver. We tried to communicate through my translator, but it was useless because he spoke in the Sicilian dialect.

Seeing Josie and her husband, Giovanni, pull up just when the bus was loading to leave again was a relief. She was five months pregnant and radiant with long dark hair and beautiful brown eyes, a natural Sicilian beauty. She had just left work, so I appreciated her unexpected trip to retrieve me.

They delivered me to my B&B and stayed until I checked in, then promised to pick me up for dinner later to meet with other family members. I downloaded pictures of my grandparents and my mother, hoping someone in the family would recognize them.

Once I settled in, I debated whether to take a nap. Travel was rough, and I felt exhausted. I opted to take a long, hot shower instead.

Invigorated, at least temporarily, I had the stamina to explore my new environment, but in what direction? The *supermercato* seemed like the best way to go. I needed a few toiletries and some wine. My GPS, set for the market, warned me that the store was closing soon. I guess that's why they call it a smartphone. The custom in Sciacca was that businesses closed from 1 to 4 p.m. Although I had enough time to accomplish my basic shopping, any other purchases had to wait. I welcomed the downtime.

Even though I had studied Sicily's history, I hadn't expected the beauty and simplicity of the island. I knew nothing about the country. As I observed the ancient architecture, I came across a building with a collapsed roof. It seemed like an intriguing subject for a picture. Long since deserted, the evidence of its inhabitants remained. The remnants of a tight community were recognizable, but the crumbling stone made it uninhabitable. Next to the 16th-century structures, others lived and thrived in unpretentious, well-maintained houses.

Along the way, I absorbed my new environment. The side streets were only wide enough for one car because everyone parked on the side, and it sometimes took some maneuvering by the oncoming traffic. The main roads were frequently packed and chaotic. I guessed that's why there were so many scooters that whooshed by. It was the preferred mode of transportation since parking was hard to come by. Cars seemed to park wherever they pleased. Some small roads ended with steps to climb, and although I'd seen some adventurous riders attempt to drive down, I didn't see anyone trying to ride up.

In the historical Centre, there were many old churches and buildings. I'd seen my share of churches and even had the honor of praying inside the Vatican, although I had to leave once the guards noticed I was sleeveless. I planned to pass this church up, except an angelic voice flowed out into the street. It compelled me to go inside the *Chiesa Del Carmine.*

When I entered, there was a young girl with her father. As he lit a candle, she walked around the podium and sang. As I became lost in the architecture of the majestic altar, her melodic tones echoed through the church. I recalled how my mom loved to sing and had inherited her father's talent for song. He only sang at weddings and family occasions, but I never had the opportunity to hear him.

Basilica Maria Santissima del Soccorso

The Lay of the Land

Sciacca is hard to describe. The air was rich with smells of the sea, and the hillside stood guard in the distance. It's a place where ordinary people live and work. There aren't many private houses, just buildings with separate balconies. The apartments were tiered from the edge of the sea up the hillside.

Along my route to the supermercato, I looked out at the Mediterranean Sea in the distance between the buildings. With so many apartments and very few private homes, I wondered if the residents had to pay real estate taxes. If not, I could see how the resources are being spread thin. Infrastructure, schools, hospitals, and law enforcement had to be maintained, but by whom?

I wasn't sure if Sciacca had a welfare system, but surely, they had to pay taxes. So, I Googled it. There are four taxes in Italy.

The IMU is a *council tax* on luxury real estate ownership, but only paid for second homes and other properties. The value and type of house determined the amount.

The TARI tax is a waste tax to finance the costs of collection and disposal, paid by all property owners in areas that produce waste. Residents pay a fixed rate based on square meters plus a variable rate based on the number of people living there.

The IUC tax is a *municipal tax* for waste and disposal. It applies to both owners and tenants.

The TASI is the *municipal tax* paid for the "Indivisible Services" to meet the lighting expenses, the maintenance of the green spaces, street cleaning, and all services provided equitably to all citizens, even tenants.

In America, the concept of real property is a symbol of wealth. Homeowners carry the burden of taxes. Even when a house has no mortgage, an annual property tax, including school taxes, is assessed. It begs the question: Do we ever actually own property?

View Walking to the supermarket.

When I returned to my room at the B&B, I opened the balcony doors to let in the cool, refreshing breeze. There was no view except the apartments across the alley. A woman came out onto her balcony with a plastic bag. She tied a knot, attached a rope, and lowered it to the street below. I realized it was trash. She probably didn't want to carry it down the stairs, a primitive system, but effective.

I set my laptop on the desk and poured a glass of wine. Outside, vendors rolled through the streets shouting their wares as they did in Brooklyn, only nowadays, they use megaphones.

Sidewalk heading down to the lower level of the Piazza

Piazza

Josie, her husband, Giovanni, and their five-year-old daughter came to pick me up for dinner at eight o'clock. The restaurant was within walking distance, and we made our way along the alleys of the town. I had thought we were going for pizza, but we entered a quaint little dining room with only four or five tables. A large group of family and friends ate, drank, and laughed. Josie greeted one of the couples, whom she hadn't seen for a while, then returned to the table and looked over the menu. Of course, it was in Italian, and I debated whether I should pull out my Google Translate camera, a handy device. If you pointed it at the text, the page magically turned to the language of your choice. Josie spared me the embarrassment and asked if I preferred fish or meat.

"We're eating fish tomorrow," she said. She knew the restaurant, so I left it up to her. We both ordered meat.

Giulia wanted pesto and pasta, but she wanted bowtie pasta instead of linguine. Restaurants in Italy don't take special orders, but Josie asked the waiter to substitute bowtie pasta. He said he'd put in a request, but it was up to the chef. When the server came back with good news, Giulia squealed with delight.

"You're going to eat it all, right?" her mother said with a wink.

Giovanni didn't speak English, and I felt terrible for him because he was out of the conversation loop, but he didn't seem to mind. Little Giulia, although she understood, only spoke Italian. Giulia, pronounced like Julia in America, didn't start with J because there was no J in the Italian language.

Soon, the dishes arrived at the table. I stared at the large plate of pesto pasta.

"Don't they have children's portions?" I asked.

"No." Josie laughed. "They don't do that here. I think we'll be helping her finish."

Shifting my attention to my plate, I noticed an array of meats, cheeses, and a cabbage leaf stuffed with eggplant marinade. I began to feel like poor Giulia. I started with the eggplant and moved to a strange piece of meat.

"Is this pork?" I asked. "It looks like bacon."

"It's like bacon, but the good kind. It isn't salted."

I took a bite and wondered why they didn't have bacon like this in the States.

View of the Port from the Piazza

After dinner, we went to the Piazza Scandaliato to meet with Giovanni's uncle, Alfredo, and his wife, Nadia, where they brought family pictures to show me and compare them to mine. I had so many questions for Caterina Corrao, the woman I originally wrote to when searching for my family. I was disappointed to hear she had died two months earlier. She lived to the age of ninety-one. When I showed my mother a picture of Caterina, she thought the facial structure resembled that of my grandfather's. If we were related, she might have been my grandfather's cousin. Giovanni's uncle and his wife were already waiting, and Josie translated our greetings.

Carousel in Piazza Angelo Scandaliato

While Giulia's father took her for a spin on the carousel, Josie spoke Italian with her brother-in-law. I gazed out on the dark sea below us, mysterious and intriguing. I wondered if my great-grandfather, Paolo Corrao, had once docked his boat there. Since he was a sailor, I assumed he had a vessel. Maybe that was why he never immigrated to the United States.

My grandfather was a fish peddler. He left Sciacca after his mother's death to make a new life.

Above us, tiny lights twinkled against the hills, like stars reaching up to the sky.

The night had a chill, and I began to feel the bite. My light sweater and thin raincoat weren't as warm as I had thought, but I kept a brave face. Giulia and her father finished the ride, and we decided to go for *gelato* to escape the cold, which was ironic but very tasty.

Alfredo, Nadia's daughter, and two of her friends joined us. The young girls were dressed in jeans and designer leather jackets. They looked like any American teenager from New York.

As I looked through Alfredo's pictures, I felt a little disappointed. I tried to find a resemblance, but it wasn't clear that these people were related. I wanted so much to be part of their beautiful family, so I kept my suspicions to myself.

Josie, Giovanni, and Giulia

View of the port from the Angelo Scandaliato Piazza

Three Levels

I awoke to the smell of fresh coffee and ventured into the communal area, where breakfast was a self-serve array of tarts, pastries, fruits, and yogurt. My eyes spotted a small dish of ham and cheese sandwiches on crusty bread. Even though I wasn't a morning eater, I took one and wrapped it in a napkin for later. The supply was limited and went fast. That, in and of itself, was enough to put a fire under me every morning to get out of bed.

Sciacca spreads over different levels, with houses and buildings running down the hillside to the harbor. The middle level is known as the Piazza Scandalato or town square. It is where most stores and restaurants cluster and where people stroll along and mingle. Something drew me back there. Trying to find the route I had taken with Josie the night before, I made my way past a small café. Just when I thought I was lost, I came around a bend, and the heart of the city opened up before me.

The piazza bustled with life. I had found the place where the older men socialized and thrived. Like a job every day, they got dressed and ate breakfast, then kissed their wives goodbye and headed to the place that gave them a purpose—to talk about family economics and politics. There was hardly a woman to be seen. I wondered what defined each group. It seemed like a social club that only they could participate in, almost cliquish. Maybe they were a family and, perhaps, neighbors who met at a specific spot and time. Or, maybe retired laborers or retired shopkeepers banded together.

The scent of *old men* reminded me of my grandfather, who lived down in the basement apartment of our house. One thing was for sure! They were all wearing his type of shoes, stylish leather slip-ons that laced up the front. When I was young, I'd seen them peeking out from under my grandfather's bed. There were also a few handmade caps like the ones worn by Italian men during the early 1900s, and they looked like those worn by newsboys in early 20th-century New York City.

Old Italian Men

From the piazza, I admired the boats in the historic fishing port and tried to figure out how to get closer. I searched for stairs but didn't see any, so I walked along the town's edge and looked out to the sea. Unless I had a car, it didn't seem possible to get down to the lower level, so I went back to taking pictures of the men in the park.

While the younger men of Sciacca started their day as construction workers or repairing boats, their grandfathers went to the town square. American men retired to play golf and work on their lawns. Italian men assembled in small groups to discuss family and world events. I found them fascinating as I watched them chat and smoke cigarettes and cigars.

Under the trees, a group played Scopa, an Italian card game whose name means "broom" because the winner sweeps the cards off the table. I contemplated taking a picture, but these men were loud and boisterous about their game. The banter became heated a few times, and it didn't take long for me to realize this was not something to take lightly.

They reminded me of my grandfather. I recalled him and his friends from the old country gathered around the concrete tables in the park across the street from our house. They looked so happy, playing Italian card games that reminded me of a mix of rummy and pinochle. My grandfather was a quiet man, but he did have a hot-blooded temper. Once, he caught one of the other card players cheating and hit him over the head with his cane.

From early morning until the sun waned, he stayed in the park, speaking in his Sicilian dialect, which was his only link to his past. I also remember when the light left his eyes. My parents decided to move to Long Island, and he had to give up his friends and the last of his Italian way of life.

The older adults of Sciacca have history locked up tight in their heads and hearts—mysteries and survival stories during Hitler and Mussolini's turbulent regimes. I'd never learn the guarded secrets they most likely took to their graves.

If only I knew Italian, I'd sit down with one of them and talk for hours. I'd ask them what they thought of American politics or capitalism compared to socialism. I'm sure they had strong opinions. Did they have family members still living in the United States? Did they care to visit them, or did they erase them from their memories?

Street Stairs at Piazza Saverio Frisia

Piazza Angelo Scandaliato

Migration

As Sicilians had carved their places in Sciacca, their hunger for America subsided. Surrounded by art, culture, and tranquility, they probably don't feel like they're missing much. As Americans, we tend to be Americentric in our thinking, believing our standards are higher than those in other countries. I'm guilty of it, but something is humbling about being in a land home to civilizations dating back to the 7th century B.C. or possibly earlier.

I took many photos, but pictures don't do it justice. They are just frozen moments, but it was all I had. Since everything changes over time, there is no one truth, and I wanted each moment to be unique--tied to emotions and senses of smell, taste, and sound.

During the early 1900s, many Italian men ventured to America to work. Unless they knew trades such as shoemaking, masonry, or tailoring, many worked as unskilled laborers in New York's Public Works Department. They dug canals, laid pavement and gas lines, built bridges, and tunneled the New York subway system. Nearly ninety percent of the laborers in New York were Italian immigrants. Some sent their money back home. Most returned to their homeland periodically, and some eventually returned home to retire.

It's incredible how much courage it took for them to travel in the most primitive conditions. I flew to Sicily in nine hours and complained about the staff not bringing water, but it sometimes took two weeks of travel in the steerage on steamships, with poor ventilation and limited space for them to get to their destination. It's hard to imagine men, women, and children crowding onto ships. Although there was a small open area, there wasn't enough room for everyone, and most ate and slept below deck, especially if there was a storm.

Their arrival provoked outrage among the Irish, more so than the influx of the Jews. Many Italian people endured prejudice against their culture. They were called Wops, Guineas, and Grease Balls. Yet they persevered. Italians sensed the resentment of those before them, but you can't stop people from migrating. New residents come with inevitable progress, which isn't necessarily good. As a town begins to shrink, even those who once welcomed progress start to worry.

Shortly after the death of his parents, Paolo and Maria, my grandfather left Sicily on the ship Berlin to join his sister, Anna, in America. She had married Salvatore Puleo, also from Sicily, and they ran a small fish market in New Jersey. They sponsored Giuseppe and gave him a job.

Anna and Giuseppe had an uncle in New York who lived in Manhattan. Giuseppe fell in love with his youngest cousin, Anna, and vowed to marry her someday, and then joined the U.S. Army.

By the time he was discharged, Anna had grown up and was already engaged to a young man named Alfred. Broken-hearted, my grandfather wished her well, but he soon got a second chance.

Giuseppe married his cousin Anna they had five daughters. Marie was the oldest, and they called her Mary —

always sweet and slightly timid. Then there was Phyllis—tough and cynical. Her nickname became Dolly. The third daughter was Anna, but she died during her first year. Shortly after, they had another girl named Anna in honor of her sister, but they nicknamed her Lucy. She was close to my mother, Jeanette, the last and youngest girl to be born.

I recalled my grandfather sitting quietly in a chair in the basement apartment my father made for him when he was in the twilight of his life. Sometimes, he let me come down to watch television with him, but I don't recall ever having an intimate conversation or connection. Maybe he couldn't relate to me.

Once, I saw a tear rolling down his cheek. It made me feel sad for him. I wondered if he was thinking about his homeland. My grandfather came from a land of beauty and simplicity. I will never know the reasons why he left Sciacca. Maybe he followed other family members drawn by the promise of a better life. When he left the place of his birth with expectations of finding happiness, he took a leap of faith.

Arco Antica Restaurant - Corso Vittorio Emanuele

Portas

There were quite a few charming restaurants around town that I wanted to try. One was alongside a cafe on Piazza Scandaliato called Ristorante Porto San Paolo, but it was closed. Just as well. After eating breakfast at the B&B and grabbing a sandwich for lunch, I wasn't too hungry. Besides, I didn't want to sit in a restaurant by myself. Although I have no problem eating out alone in the States, it somehow didn't seem right in Sciacca. I didn't know the language and couldn't communicate with anyone.

Josie invited me for *Sunday Sauce* with the family. How fitting, since the title of my book is *Sauce on Sunday*.

Church Door – Piazza del Carmine

Some women are obsessed with shoes, but for me, it's doors. I've had a love of doors all my life: pocket doors, French doors, carved wooden doors—any unique doors. I even considered learning how to make them, but I didn't have a woodshop.

The doors I love most are the ones still in use. In years past, Porte Palermo was closed at certain times, the town's way of controlling traffic in and out of the square.

Porto di Palermo

Dolce Vita

If there is one thing that my mother drummed into me, it's that you should never show up at someone's house without a gift or some sweet dessert. I had to find something quick, so I sought a local bakery. Before I even entered the shop, I inhaled the sweet enticements. Of course, there was the ever-popular *Cannoli*, tube-shaped shells of fried pastry dough filled with sweetened, creamy ricotta. Then there were the *Sfogliatella*, native to Campania, the shell-shaped flaky dough resembling stacked leaves stuffed with ricotta filling. Among the *Zeppoles*, *Tiramisu*, and cream-filled *Profiteroles* with chocolate sauce, I spotted one of my favorites. *Pasticcotti* – little tarts filled with vanilla or chocolate custard.

Usually, I avoid sugar because diabetes runs in my family. My grandfather was diagnosed in his early fifties, as both of my great-grandparents developed retinopathy, a condition in which tiny blood vessels inside the retina are damaged by diabetes. My grandmother ended up taking care of them when they went blind.

It wasn't hard for me to avoid Italian desserts, especially since I left New York. A bakery was on every corner in those days, and patrons lined up down the block on weekends. The taste of fresh poppy seed rolls remains in my memory, which we ate with plenty of butter. The bakers had a hard time keeping up with the demand.

During my last trip to Long Island, I was surprised to see the bare shelves.

"Where are all your pastries?" I asked.

"They have to be ordered ahead of time."

During the eighties, people became health-conscious and stopped eating a lot of sweets. I imagined they had a lot of waste.

My mother wasn't a baker, but I'll never forget a rare moment and one that has burned into my memories, one Christmas. She and my father scurried around the kitchen together. They were baking—not some *Medigan* (Pronounced Merde de Cane - the Italian word for non-Italian, which means dog shit.) pre-packaged mix, but actual cookies, from scratch. Trays of anisette cookies and Struffoli, little dough balls smothered in honey and decorated with colorful candy sprinkles.

In Italy, I peered into full shelves of Italian pastries and authentic butter cookies that melt in your mouth, not the ones you buy at the supermarket, made with lard. I wanted to try every one of them. I had my eyes on two pastries. If I got to taste at least one, I would die happy. The problem occurred when I left with my special sweets. I peered into each pastry shop, tempted to get one of everything.

With a couple of hours to kill, I returned my pastries to the B&B and then took another long walk through the side streets. Since it was Sunday, most of the stores closed. I noted a few establishments and planned to return, but there were so many shops and streets. The city wasn't large, but the chances of finding the same shops again might prove difficult. I've had the same frustration whenever I walked around New York City. Even with well-written directions and landmarks, I couldn't find the shops again. It was like they fell off the map.

Sauce or Gravy

Josie and her future sister-in-law, Cristina, came to pick me up for dinner, but parked at the end of the road. I was wearing heels and carefully navigated the uneven pavement to get to them. She lived in the country, about twenty miles from the town center.

Before we went upstairs, Josie said she had to pick some parsley from the garden, so we walked around to the back of the building. The smell of herbs filled the air. Fresh herbs have a more pungent scent than those sitting on shelves in plastic jars. Five-year-old Giulia spotted a cat on one of the lower patios and ran to pet it. I was missing Riley, so I was right behind her.

"This is one of my father's apartments," Josie said. "It's empty." She laughed. "Maybe you can come back and rent it for the summer."

"Hmm. I don't know. My cat is a good traveler, but he's never been on a plane. Besides, it's such a long flight. He's fourteen now. I don't think he'd make it."

The view from Josie's balcony was panoramic. One side faced the Mediterranean, and the other faced the hills. As I sipped my wine, I looked down into the vegetable garden and enjoyed the warm sunshine on my face. I noticed frames on both sides of the garden, which I immediately recognized as a trellis for grapes, but nothing was growing yet. It reminded me of my neighbors back on Long Island. They came from Italy and bought the house next to ours. Within a month, their yard was full of vegetables. By summer, they sat on a long table under trellises laden with fragrant grapes. The scent drifted into our yard, along with plenty of bees. Even in Brooklyn, Italian immigrants grew grapes for their homemade wine. They set up trellises on the rooftops if they didn't have yard space.

You have to love a man who cooks. Giovanni was the chef for "Sauce on Sunday." There was no meat in the pot but lots of basil, salt, and pepper. I asked what the secret was for a great sauce, and he said fresh tomatoes, but only if they were in season. Fresh tomatoes? I laughed. You just can't find that at the local supermarket back home. The tomatoes in most produce sections didn't taste very good at all. Most weren't naturally ripened. Aside from that, all the pesticides and fertilizers used in gardening have changed something. Americans had given up taste for aesthetics. Everything had to be the same, and God forbid there was a bug in the produce. Unless a local farm was nearby, people in America relied on canned tomatoes.

Americans sometimes debate whether it's called sauce or gravy. I was confused until Giovanni explained, "If it has no meat, it's a sauce. If it does, then it's gravy." It all made sense to me. When you think about it, brown gravy is made from turkey, chicken, or beef drippings. Gravy needs to simmer for a long time—the longer, the better.

Every Sunday, my mother would pull out the old silver pot handed down from her mother and simmer the tomatoes. The smell of meatballs frying in the skillet filled the air. Two were set aside in a dish for my father, who preferred them without gravy. My mother's gravy always tasted better than mine. She said the secret was to use a lot of eggs in the meatballs.

"What's a lot?" I asked, but I never did get a straight answer. Meat or no meat—it was delicious anyway.

Course after course found its way to the table. So much food! I had to taste everything. When it came time for dessert, I did try one of the pastries on my "cravings list," but Giulia gobbled up the other. Oh well, one out of two wasn't bad.

Thank goodness Josie and Cristina suggested that we go for a walk afterward. With little Giulia in her stroller, we walked down to the resort village, which was gated. The guard seemed to know Josie and let us in. She booked many tourists into the resort at the Dedalo Tour Company, where she worked.

The path forked in three directions, all leading to different club resorts. We turned to the right, leading to Josie's favorite, the Club Cala Regina, an all-inclusive, four-star beachfront resort. I immediately thought of my cousins from Staten Island. They'd love this resort by the sea.

Sciacca isn't a major tourist town, but it has all the makings of one. Most Americans ventured to Mexico or the Caribbean, but the French had found this vacation spot, little known to the rest of the world. Every summer, they booked the rooms to capacity.

It was a perfect Sunday. Josie's family instantly adopted me. Giovanni's brother and fiancée, Christina, invited me to their house for an upcoming holiday barbecue. Before they drove me back to the B&B, I told Josie about Vincenzo, the man who, coincidentally, had texted me on WhatsApp that morning to ask if I had arrived in Sciacca. I had forgotten all about him until then. He, too, had responded to one of my letters and contacted me on Facebook. I mentioned where I was staying and suggested we get together for lunch before leaving. When I looked at the message history, there was a picture of his grandmother, Caterina, who looked frail and close to death. When I mentioned her name to Josie at dinner the previous night, she reminded me that Caterina had died. I was getting confused. Was this the same Caterina?

Josie wanted to check Vincenzo's Facebook profile, so I pulled it up on my phone.

"Oh no!" she said.

"What's wrong?"

Sauce or Gravy | 57

"This is Giovanni's cousin. He's a *bad* man," Josie said. "Don't meet with him."

I promised not to have further contact with Vincenzo. When I returned to my room, I pulled up his page and scrolled down his timeline. I viewed sexually explicit ads, inappropriate content, and offensive comments, so I immediately clicked 'unfriend.'

Cala Maria Resort

Piazza Saverio Friscia

Holiday

Holidays are taken very seriously in Sciacca, especially religious holidays. Twice a year, the city's patron saint, Our *Lady of Distress,* is carried in procession throughout the city streets by more than one hundred barefoot sailors. The statue is adorned with jewels of gold, silver, and coral. This tradition dates back to 1626 when *the righteous* were cured of the Black Death, known as the Plague.

As I took my morning walk, I stumbled across the official ceremony. It was Festa della Liberazione, a national holiday commemorating the end of the Italian Civil War and Nazi occupation during World War II. It reminded me of Memorial Day, all pageantry and patriotism, followed by a celebration of food and drink. I'm sure the residents of Sciacca welcomed the day off from work, but it left me to wander around the town, peeking into windows with signs that said CHIUSO.

In search of an open store to buy a gift, I could only find a panificio, where I bought a fresh loaf of bread with sesame seeds. The only other place that was open was a discount store. Go figure! It gave me an idea. Thinking of the bag of candy I had brought from home, I bought a cute little box and filled it with the Dove dark chocolates. Then, I found a toy store the day before and bought Giulia a small doll. It was a habit of mine to spoil children in my family. I loved to see their happy little faces when they received an unexpected gift.

The chocolates and the little light-up pixie I'd bought for Giulia were a hit. Sitting around the table with Giovanni's family, his mother and father told stories of long-lost relatives, all in Italian. I couldn't understand a word, but Josie stopped occasionally to translate.

Christina, my host, grilled some Romanian meatballs, one of her family's specialties. They were shaped more like hot dogs and marinated overnight in beer — an acquired taste, but they were tasty.

Christina and Giovanni were the head grillers on the roof. I had to laugh. It was nothing like the backyard barbecues in the States, especially on Long Island.

On weekends or holidays, smoke billowed from backyard barbecues, and the smell of hot dogs and hamburgers cooking filled the air.

After stuffing myself for two days during Sunday dinner at Josie's, I was trying hard not to overeat. It began well enough. There was a wide variety of fresh vegetables and olives on the table. Giulia whined that she was hungry. Her grandmother, Maria Corrao, offered her some finocchio, or fennel as I knew it, a celery-like vegetable that smelled like licorice. My grandfather used to say fennel was good for digestion.

Giulia didn't seem to have a problem and gobbled down two stalks, so I tried it and decided that I would buy some when I returned home.

There was so much food. It started with tuna bruschetta—grilled bread rubbed with olive oil and garlic and topped with fresh tuna and chopped tomatoes, basil, salt, and pepper.

Sciacca is the oily fish capital of the world and still has many canneries that process fresh sardines, mackerel, herring, and tuna. Memories of my childhood flooded back. We ate a lot of tuna in my house, but I never thought about where it came from. It seemed like an American staple, especially the way my mother prepared it—with plenty of mayonnaise. She always hid a can, along with snacks, somewhere other than the kitchen cabinet. My siblings and I used to go on secret food hunts. It was like striking gold when we found a treasured can of tuna under her mattress or on the windowsill in her room.

Whenever I opened a can of tuna, my cat Riley came running to the kitchen. No matter how quiet I tried to be, he always knew. I'd turn around, and he'd be sitting right behind me, waiting expectantly for his share.

Mangiare, mangiare! Sicilians sure seemed to love fattening you up, and I complied. Although I wasn't in the habit of eating dessert, I refused to pass up the cream-filled pastry smothered in chocolate.

Stuffed to the gills, I felt my dress tighten. Just the smell seemed to add extra pounds to my waistline. *Maybe I'll skip breakfast in the morning.* Hmm!

Rooftop Barbecue

Via Conzo

Remnants of the Past

My stomach was full from the day before, and I skipped breakfast. Besides, Josie and Giovanni were picking me up to go out for pizza. Somehow, I needed to work off enough calories to be hungry by evening, so I took a long walk.

    I planned to walk down to the port and check out the boats, but before that, I wanted to feel the pulse of the town where my grandfather spent his youth. I imagined him as a child riding a bike or playing with his cousins, and wondered what grade he reached in school. I'm sure he didn't stay past the fifth or sixth grade because most children had to work from an early age. I wanted to see where he started his educational journey. Earlier, I had searched the internet for schools and later found out that, in the early 1900s, children attended school at the Basilica Maria del Soccorso. The school was only a short distance from the harbor. It looked like a fortress with steel fencing around the perimeter. Except for some colorful emblems on one window, the sound of children's laughter was the only indication that it was a school. It looked more like a barracks than a school. The architecture didn't match the rest of the town.

Via Delle Dogane

As I headed toward the harbor, I came across an old bridge with crumbling bricks. Things like this interested me more than tourist monuments because it was evidence of a time long gone. That world no longer existed, but the remnants would continue long after I was gone.

Remnants of a once-busy industrial market clung to the shoreline. Due to its quiet nature and size, it isn't one of the top ten places for tourists to visit unless they are on an ancestral journey. Most travelers frequent places like Palermo or Taormina.

Via Antonio Gramsci

Memories are not concrete; they fade. It's their nature. I didn't trust my memory, so I frequently stopped to jot down notes along my journeys. I felt the need to record everything of interest. I observed buildings that once housed generations of families, maybe even mine. Others had passed this way and taken with them different recollections, depending on their moods, memories, or even the weather.

Once I finish my book, I hope other Americans will read it and get something from my perceptions, even if we are alike in our Italianness.

Pastificio Saccense Pasta Mill

The Harbor

Sciacca is the second-largest fishing port in Sicily. Hundreds of pounds of fish are caught every day and delivered to the cannery. They are packed in oil and then exported throughout Sicily and the world. Purse seine nets, drawn into the shape of a bag using a line along the bottom of the net like the drawstring of a purse, catch schooling fish like sardines, mackerel, and tuna. The fishing nets are controversial because they encircle both targeted and unwanted fish, creating a staggering amount of seafood waste.

Because of Sciacca's strategic position, the Greeks and Carthaginians fought to dominate the territory. It didn't become a prominent city until the Romans conquered it. Sciacca retained its prosperity until the fall of the Roman Empire.

The ancient influences of Greek, Roman, Arabic, and even North African cultures have touched Sicily in the past. Sciacca has suffered destructive invasions by the Vandals, the Goths, and the Byzantines. Later, hermit monks Christianized the people of Sicily and lived in caves on Mount Kronio, also known as Mount San Calogero. Even the Arabs marked the history of Sciacca when they expanded to eastern Sicily and conquered "Thermae." They built massive walls and the famous "Old Castle," which has withstood the test of time.

Charles Bourbone of Spain established a Sea Consulate, making it a hub for Palermo trade by land and sea. During my grandfather's youth in the 1870s, Sciacca bustled with industry. That might be why my great-grandfather left Palermo to reside there.

From the harbor, I had a view of the piazza, and the upper level of the town housed the castle and many old churches and buildings.

Groups of people were herded off a tour bus. I felt grateful that I wasn't one of them. For me, it wasn't an enjoyable way to see a city—cramming things in just to say you'd been there. I'd much rather take my time and absorb the environment.

Lega Navale

Boats creaked and rocked back and forth at the marina as the water slapped against their sides. The heady scent of marine life mingled with the smell of motor oil.

Three young men were fishing. I asked if they spoke English because younger people seemed more inclined to speak English. They didn't, but one spoke French. Since I had studied French in college, I thought I could communicate. He told me that fishing was difficult, but they tried.

"Oui. C'est difficile!" I said.

Seeing that I understood what he was saying, he began to talk faster. He started speaking at a level that was over my head, so I moved on.

Since it was still morning and socially acceptable to order a cappuccino, I decided to stop at the cafe. The gated marina had a lock reserved only for marina staff and those who owned boats. As an outsider, I had to settle for taking pictures through the gate.

Just as I was about to walk away, two men approached the gate with a key. They nodded for me to enter, a golden opportunity to have a cappuccino by the sea. Though my Italian was spotty at best, I managed to communicate with some Coast Guard staff.

"Why Sciacca?" one asked.

"My grandfather… born in Sciacca," I said. "A fisherman."

"Ah… Un pescatore!"

I nodded because it sounded like un pêcheur, a French fisherman. I was starting to see connections between the Romance languages of Europe.

We talked in broken Italian and hand gestures, and I told them about my great-grandfather, Paolo, also a sailor.

Via Gale di Garaffe

The Boat Yard

Revved up on caffeine and local culture, I forgot about my aching feet and returned to the piazza. Skilled boat crafters still build small and medium-sized boats in Sciacca's modest shipyard. Passing the discarded vessels was oddly fascinating. My mind wandered back through the years, and I imagined them in full glory.

Despite the rundown structures, well-maintained apartments stood next to boarded-up buildings of trade. Not that the many roaming cats were complaining. They had plenty of fish and mice.

Largo S. Paolo

Josie had mentioned that people took on pets only to abandon them in the streets. She thought it was unfortunate, especially for the dogs, because they were usually starved or hit by cars. I didn't dare tell her some people in America did the same things and sometimes worse.

I thought of my Riley back home. My daughter had brought home a pregnant cat, and even though I protested, I caved in and kept one kitten. He had a chronic ear infection caused by mites, which left him weak and sickly. I couldn't take the chance that he'd end up on death row at the animal shelter, so he became mine.

Finally, I found the stairs that led from the piazza to the harbor — the same ones I searched for on my second day. They were hidden behind the carousel.

Vicolo Galleria

Piazza Scandaliato

The Boat Yard | 73

Spiaggia

Around a rocky border, sandy beaches hugged the coast to either side of the town, but getting down was challenging. The color of the sea seemed to shift from blue to aqua, magnified by the sun's rays.

Looking down at the shore, I saw what seemed to be a grave marker at first. I thought it was an odd place to bury someone, so I took a picture and translated the words.

The stone on the left said, "Dio ha scosso il mondo con un bimbo non con una bomba; God shook the world with a baby, not a bomb." The stone on the right said "Tutti pensano a cambiare l'umanita e nessuno pensa a cambiare se stesso."

Everyone thinks of changing humanity, and no one thinks about changing himself.

Via Enrico Ghezzi

There was also a monument for the Dixmude, an airship built for the Imperial German Navy and given to France as a reparation after the First World War. Recommissioned in the French Navy, it exploded in mid-air on 21 December 1923 off the coast of Sicily.

I cut through a small park and noticed what looked like a cactus plant. Not my favorite. I wondered why it was growing in Sicily. The plant was laden with fruit, so I took a closer look. Small and wrinkled, they looked like figs.

The two main varieties cultivated were the "Italian White," yellowish-green in color, and the "Italian Black," a deep purple when ripe. I'd seen many figs, especially when my grandfather was alive, but I never had a taste for the Mediterranean fruit. It looked like a prune, something my grandfather ate to stay regular. Yet, there were many fig trees grown on Brooklyn rooftops. Italians love their figs. They even took shoots with them to plant in America.

I later found out they weren't figs at all and, indeed, not a cactus plant. It was a prickly pear tree.

"Can you eat them?" I asked.

"Well, yes, but they are wild and a little bitter in taste."

I returned to watch the fishing boats pull into the harbor. The smell of decaying fish from the previous day's catch mingled with the salty air.

Trucks and vans of all sizes patiently awaited the day's catch. The fishermen secured the mooring lines and unloaded trays of sardines, shrimp, and crayfish on shaved ice. Some of the tuna weighed over 70 kg, and took two men to lift them ashore.

Vendors and restaurateurs hustled to negotiate prices and load the fish onto their trucks.

Via Giuseppe Licata

Pistachio Cream

Sicily is well-known for ceramic art made from clay mined from the valleys and mountains, mixed with silicates. Museum-quality sculptures and mosaic scenes were created and designed in beautiful colors around the town. The "souvenir mission" was upon me, but I didn't have money to waste, and I had very little room in my suitcase. I walked along Corso Vittorio Emanuele, where several shops were selling colorful plates and tiles. Even if I packed them carefully, I was afraid they'd break. Besides, I'd probably be able to order them online.

I wanted to take home a taste of Sicily. Luckily, I found a small shop that sold leather bracelets in various colors that read, "I Love Sicily." I bought eight, then found a shop selling pistachio cream and decided to buy it as *my* souvenir. The jar was heavy, but after tasting the fresh croissants exploding with pistachio every morning, how could I resist? I loved pistachios, but wasn't aware they grew them near Mt. Etna in Sicily's Bronte area. They are harvested by hand every two years and considered green gold, which explains why they're so expensive.

Via Maglienti Friscia

Comune di Sciacca

What's in a Name

The *Comune di Sciacca* loomed before me, and I was tempted to go inside, although it wouldn't do me much good. For one thing, I didn't speak the language. Besides, many people have warned me that government workers are known for being unmotivated. Josie said that once, the mayor tried to fix the system. He was voted in during a conservative swing and a desire for change. The mayor fired all the non-productive people working in city jobs. He whipped things into shape but ruffled so many feathers that he was voted out at the next election, and everything went back to the way it was. It reminded me of the turbulent climate back home. Republicans rallied for President Trump to take office and change the country. When he won, people were disillusioned. Even the conservatives second-guessed their devotion to some of Trump's methods. My own family was Republican, but only because it was economically preferable on Long Island at the time. The ideology was so embedded that my brother enticed my sister to get our eighty-four-year-old mother to the voting booth by bribing her with a free dinner afterward.

The name Corrao is reasonably common in Sciacca. There's even a family crest. As it traveled to America, the spelling sometimes changed. The correct Italian pronunciation is Corrao, with a rolling r. My grandmother's parents spelled it Currao. I don't know why. Maybe because some census workers didn't understand the accent and accidentally spelled it Currao, or perhaps my relatives purposely changed it to hide that my grandmother and grandfather were cousins. To make things more complicated, my aunt used the spelling Currao, too, which caused me confusion when I first started researching my family. Another puzzling fact was that even if the firstborn is a girl, she is named after the paternal grandfather in Italian customs. For example, Giuseppe, if male, or Giuseppa, if female. No wonder I kept going in circles when I researched my ancestry. I had come to find my ancestors, but it wasn't such an easy task. These were my people, yet the distance of one hundred years had created a veil.

Coming all this way and being unable to access the records housed inside was frustrating. I had an inside contact—something most people didn't have. Giovanni's father offered to help find information about my great-grandfather, Paolo Corrao. I gave him a copy of his birth certificate.

That innocent statement about my heritage while having coffee with some friends compelled me to research my ancestors, all the way back to my great-great-great-grandfather, Pasquale Corrao. I created a family website and posted information as I discovered it. So, I signed up for a free week's trial on one of the popular ancestry sites. Still, I found nothing to bridge the way back to Italy. Then, I discovered the Genealogy Society at my local library. There, I met a woman experienced in digging up the roots of her people. Adeline offered to help me.

One Sunday, while we were going through digitalized microfilm records on her computer, and found my grandfather's birth certificate. I discovered the names of my great-grandparents, Paolo Corrao and Maria Colletti. I tried to locate their birth certificates, hoping that maybe my great-grandfather had brothers and sisters who remained in Italy, but I hit a dead end.

They left no trail for me to follow, and the path seemed to go cold until it led me to search genealogy.com, a website dedicated to researching family history and message boards. I googled the genealogy site and entered my family name. That's where I found a post from a woman named Marianna. She was also looking for information about our family. I was doubtful because she mentioned a second sister, and I only knew of Anna, who accompanied my grandfather to America. I replied to Marianna's message, but didn't expect to hear from her because the original posting was six years old.

Monte San Calogero

It was my last day in the village, and I felt sad. The journey opened my eyes to many different facets of Sciacca. I could spend the rest of my days sitting in the park like my grandfather and never tire of my ancestors' seaside village. I will leave my heart here, knowing I will return to claim it.

Josie and her husband picked me up for pizza at Pizzeria La Grande Valle with Alfredo and Nadia. Before we went to the restaurant, Giovanni drove to the natural steam caves on the slopes of Monte San Calogero to show me the thermal spas. Although it was dark, I got a feel for the site and was able to take some clear pictures of the town below. The stars sparkled against the night sky and seemed just out of reach of my fingers. I imagined the ancient Greeks and Romans. What did they think when they looked out at the universe? Did they count the stars? Long after they died, others took a front-row view of this beautiful arena.

We were on our way to the Pizzeria la Grande Valle. I wasn't particularly hungry because I had a late lunch, but I was anxious to taste authentic Sicilian pizza.

"You're going to love this pizza," Josie said. "It's the best in Sciacca."

How different can it be?

There was so much food. Large individual pizzas came to the table, along with a mound of French fries with mayonnaise. I didn't know how I was going to eat it all. Then I thought, *tonight is the last night to stuff. Just enjoy.* Josie was right. The pizza was delicious, the best I'd had since I was a young girl in Brooklyn. It was the real thing.

Since I had left New York, my expectations diminished. In Georgia and Florida, it always disturbed me when I saw a sign that said *New York Style Pizza*. Some people think good pizza needs to be loaded with sauce and cheese, but the best pizza has a delicate blend of ingredients.

No matter how I tried, I couldn't put a dent in the pie in front of me. The waitress came and asked if we wanted a box.

"No, that's okay," Josie said.

I watched with dismay as that yummy pizza traveled through the double doors of the back kitchen. That made me feel even worse, but there was no way I could eat it unless I wanted pizza for breakfast, and I had already set my sights on one more pistachio cream croissant.

There are many accounts of the origin of pizza. The word "pizza," derived from the Latin word picea, means "the burning of bread using an oven." Most people believe pizza is an invention of Italians, and so did I for a long time. Then, I met world-renowned artisan Chef Lippe. At the Vero Beach Wine and Film Festival, I saw him cooking pasta in a large, hollowed-out wheel of Parmesan cheese. Once the festival was over, I saw Lippe again at the after-party. He sat beside me, and we had a pleasant conversation over a glass or two of Cabernet. Somehow, the conversation turned to pizza.

"Do you know who created pizza?" he asked.

"The Romans?"

He laughed. "Most people think that, but you might be surprised that it was the Egyptians. They used the cooked dough as a dish to hold the food and reused it after each meal."

"Didn't it get moldy?"

"No, because the climate was hot, and it dried out the dough. The Romans didn't know this, so they ate it, and the pizza was born."

I thought Chef Lippe was pulling my leg, so I researched it online. Sure enough, I found an article, *History of Pizza*, which supported most of his claims. Featured on a pizza supplier's webpage, they cited the history of the flatbread, which was a poor man's substitute for a plate or utensil.

To my surprise, I received a message from Marianna, a third cousin. She was the great-granddaughter of Anna Corrao, my grandfather's sister. She said she had the birth certificates of my grandfather and his two sisters. *Two sisters?* I only knew of one, Anna, who accompanied my grandfather to America. As it turns out, Maria, the second sister, had married and had nine children. During her ancestry research, Marianna found the family members of Maria. Most were second and third cousins who still lived in Sciacca, though some had settled in America.

La Famiglia Paolo Corrao and Maria

Close Encounter

The Autolinee Gallo bus ran irregularly throughout the day and took around an hour and forty minutes. Since I got off at the wrong stop on my way to Sciacca, I had to figure out the location of the return bus to Palermo. Luckily, the buses departed from across the street from the travel agency where Josie worked. It was alongside a little park called the Villa Comunale.

I planned to take a later bus and stay as long as possible, but my flight from Palermo was leaving at four, and I didn't want to risk it. If the unforeseen were to happen, I'd miss my plane. So, I decided to leave earlier. I popped into Josie's office to say goodbye, then dragged my suitcase to the corner. All I had to do was find the right bus. I already had a round-trip ticket.

While I was waiting, I sat on the bench near the park and chewed on some fennel I had purchased from a fresh vegetable stand on the side of the road.

A man came up, and I moved my stuff, thinking he wanted to sit.

"Palermo?" he asked.

"Si," I said and smiled.

He only spoke Italian but tried desperately to communicate. "Il mio nome è Angelo."

I pulled out my translator, and he quickly typed a message, but with his Sicilian dialect, the phrases came out all wrong. I still got the gist of what he was saying.

"Can I drive you to Palermo in my car?"

"No, grazie," I said and showed him my ticket.

He wrote his phone number on a slip of paper. I didn't want to be rude, so I gave him a business card with only my email address.

The bus arrived on time, and the stranger grabbed my suitcase and loaded it with the other baggage, then kissed me on both cheeks. "Ciao."

"Ciao," I said and scrambled onto the safety of the bus.

Sitting comfortably in my seat, I looked out the side window. To my horror, Angelo from the bus stop was waving and using sign language for me to call him.

I willed the bus to move. It rolled forward, but the man ran beside it for a moment until we picked up speed and left him behind.

Santa Margherita di Belice

Twenty minutes later, the bus pulled into the next town, Santa Margherita di Belice, to let more people off. I took out my camera to shoot a few photos of the old ruins. Just before the bus pulled away, I saw Angelo again. He stood outside, gesturing that he would see me at the station when I arrived in Palermo. Oh, crap!

Situations like this always fill me with anxiety. I didn't know Angelo and was too scared to take the risk of sharing a meal or drink. Besides, he had terrible breath. I wondered what dental coverage was like in Sicily.

As much as I enjoyed seeing my grandfather's ancestral town, I was disappointed I never found the cemetery. There were no computers to use for such purposes. Any records would have been handwritten in a book back then. It was impossible unless I had weeks or months to go through the records.

I thought about my mother. If only I had considered making the trip ten years earlier, I would have taken her along. But since her stroke, that dream was never fulfilled.

The countryside whizzed past my window with rolling hills of farmland rich with produce, all planted in neatly lined rows. I imagined the past and present people living and cultivating the land.

The bus traveled through the Valley of Belice, where, in 1968, an earthquake with a magnitude of 5.5 intensity destroyed most of the town, leaving only the ruins of the medieval castle and a statue of St. Catherine.

Approximately four hundred people had died.

Some prominent families pressured government officials to rebuild on a slope 385 meters above sea level, and the town was renamed Salaparuta. Cows and goats dotted the landscape between olive groves and vineyards with little evidence of the disaster.

When the bus pulled into the Balsamo station in Palermo, I looked to see if Angelo was there. He wasn't. I was relieved and followed the passengers to wait by the bus for the driver to give us our luggage. I looked up, and there he was again. Fumbling with the translator on my phone, I typed a message saying that I was sorry but was meeting my boyfriend. His face seemed to fall, and he quickly made Italian apologies for bothering me. I watched him walk away, feeling a little embarrassed for him.

As I wandered through Palermo, I stopped to admire the billboards of handsome Italian men sporting the latest fashion styles. I found the contrast striking when it came to the way men dress in Sicily. It seemed like those male models had jumped off the boards. While Sciacca was more laid back with an older population, Palermo thrived with young, vibrant men. The majority were impeccably dressed, from their well-groomed hairstyles to their Bruno Magli shoes. It put most American men to shame, especially those who never gave up their shorts, sneakers, and sweats.

The women of Palermo didn't have the same fashion sense as the men. But they made up for their lack of style with their unique beauty. There was no way to compete with such elegance. For the first time, I felt old.

I dropped my luggage at the apartment and headed to the supermercato. Along the way, I did a little window shopping. Even though my feet hurt, I was on a mission. I couldn't stop thinking about the ravioli I had purchased and cooked in the apartment on my first night in Palermo. They rolled around my mind like ravioli in boiling water. Replicating my exact order, I anticipated an excellent dinner. I bought the same ravioli, the same jar of tomato sauce, the same bottle of wine, plus yogurt for the morning.

Halfway back to the apartment, my feet gave out, and I purchased a bus ticket. Although I got on the right bus, it didn't stop where I thought it would. Two blocks, three blocks, and four blocks later, I got off and had to walk back to where it had passed—so much for saving my feet. I climbed six flights of stairs, visions of pasta and wine driving me on.

Feeling a bit indulgent, I ate the whole package of ravioli and drank the bottle of wine. I was sick all night with *agita*!

I felt a pang of sadness as I left for the airport in the morning. Toni called for a taxi to pick me up at the station across the street.

Via Orologio - Palermo

Feline Persuasion

When I disembarked from the plane, I thought about Riley. I imagined his little furry face staring out the window, waiting for me to come home. He'd wistfully look out into the field next to my apartment as birds and squirrels darted back and forth.

As I exited the airport, I breathed in the scent of the ocean in the breeze. It felt good to be back in Florida. Searching for my car, I walked from one row to the next. Since it was dark when I parked it, I couldn't remember where it was. Frustrated, I searched for my vehicle. Finally, I spotted the sporty white Genesis. I practically ran, the wheels of my suitcase lifting off the ground as I went. Clicker in hand, I pressed it, expecting the familiar beep of the trunk release. Nothing! I clicked again. Still, the trunk remained closed. I had to open the car door manually with the key. At least that worked. I pressed the button to start the engine. Nothing! Something was wrong. The headlight switch was in the on position. The battery was dead.

I frantically searched the glove compartment for my AAA card, but then I remembered it was in my wallet, which I left at home. Surely, this has happened to other travelers. I left the suitcase in the car and searched the parking lot for someone to help me. I saw an airport staff member rolling around in a golf cart four rows over. I tried to head him off, but he was too fast, and I ran around the parking lot, trying to get his attention. The Florida heat slowed me down, and I headed back inside the airport. The terminal guard chuckled when I told him about my predicament. "You wouldn't believe how many people come home to a dead battery," he said, trying to make me feel better. "I'll call someone to jump you."

An hour later, I was rolling along the highway and on my way home to Riley.

I scooped him up in my arms the minute I walked through the door. Cats' thoughts and emotions are not simple to read. If he was angry that I left him, I couldn't tell. His eyes held a faraway look, and he was emotionally distant. I think he was glad to see me, but he looked leery. I'd have to work on getting his trust again — planning to spoil him rotten.

He stayed by my side all night but remained emotionally distant until morning. When we first moved into the apartment, I designated the spot under the bathroom sink as his toilet and set up the kitty litter. I'd wake to the slamming cabinet door in the bathroom. He was quite capable of opening the cabinet door whenever he needed to do his business, but lately, he didn't even try.

I dragged myself out of bed and found the cabinet door already open. It was. Riley learned to slam the door to get my attention.

Maybe it took him that long to process the information that his old routine was at hand. He wanted to go out and made it clear that he expected to. I contemplated his desire but decided it was best to keep him inside, mainly because he had a sneezing fit whenever I let him out. Besides, it was getting bothersome to stumble down the apartment stairs at 6 a.m. every morning. We were both getting too old for that.

With a low guttural sound, he said, "I wanna-go-owwwt," in cat talk. It wasn't the first time Riley told me this. I always knew he was an extraordinary feline, but English? Once, I suspected he might be an alien. Maybe it was the shape of his eyes. They were similar to the sci-fi movies that depict beings from outer space.

You could say we had an understanding. I knew which meow meant that he was hungry, which meow meant he was annoyed. I knew when he wanted me to hold him on my lap and when he wanted to be left alone. He seemed to know me pretty well, too.

Riley jumped onto the windowsill and took turns looking out, then at me. Not even a refreshing bowl of cold milk would satisfy him.

"Sorry, buddy," I said. "I can't afford for you to get sick."

Riley was the worst and the best cat I ever owned. He disagreed with my decision and paced back and forth in front of my computer. In a fit of anger, he tried to knock things off my desk. When I told him to stop, he looked at me and pushed my pen with his paw as if to say, "Who's the boss?"

Tony's Di Napoli - Manhattan

Reunion

During her ancestry research, Marianna, the great-granddaughter of Anna Corrao, found the family members of Nonna Maria. Most were third cousins from Sciacca, but some lived in America. We planned a cousins' reunion in Manhattan. At first, only six of us were getting together, but the number kept growing.

It was a hot and steamy August night when sixteen cousins and their families met at New York's Tony's di Napoli Restaurant. We all had one thing in common. We were the descendants of three siblings who were separated years ago.

On Giuseppe Corrao's side were my sister, Daine, my cousins Linda, Jane, Billy, and me.

Anna Corrao Puleo's daughter, Marie, Marianna, and two nephews, Lewis and Joe, were there.

Maria Corrao Ruffo's two granddaughters, Rita and her sister Brigida, attended.

Rita lived in Lake Ronkonkoma on Long Island. My sister lived in that same town. To think—I had spent many days and weeks there. We might have crossed paths with Rita for years without knowing we were related. The moment I laid eyes on her, I felt a connection. Everyone commented on how we looked like sisters.

We sat around a large table, eating, laughing, and talking. Families from Manhattan, Long Island, Staten Island, and New Jersey came together. It was surreal looking at all the faces, knowing the same blood flowed among us. The grandchildren of three siblings, separated during their youth, sitting around a table after a lifetime apart?

Growing up, I had always felt different from my schoolmates, especially the blonde-haired, blue-eyed girls who seemed to look down on my Mediterranean skin tone and brown eyes as if I were "less than." Maybe if I hadn't been disconnected from my family heritage, I would have had the confidence other Italian girls seemed to share. I never really knew what it meant to be Italian, except for that Sunday ritual, macaroni and meatballs. Genetics aside, I had no real connection—no anchor.

Rita told me that she was going to Sciacca in September. It whetted my appetite for Italy again, and I immediately contemplated my next trip to Sicily.

Dumped in Milan

With only one month until my second trip to Sciacca, I didn't have too much time to learn to speak Italian. I downloaded a language course and practiced for an hour every day. Rita was scheduled to arrive the day after I did, and we were going to search for gravesites. She was traveling with her sister, Pina, and I was excited to meet her and their other sister, Maria. Since they were born in Sciacca, they spoke the dialect fluently. My great aunt Maria had long since passed away, but had nine children. That was a lot of grandchildren, and I was going to meet them. Surely, they'd have pictures, hopefully of their Nonna and her siblings. Perhaps they'd even have some of my great-grandfather, Paolo, and great-grandmother, Maria.

I noticed Riley sitting at the edge of my bed. He was staring at the wall, drool dripping from his mouth. I knew this to mean that an animal was in pain. *Oh no! Not again.* It was stressful enough to leave him, and just like last time, he decided to make it harder by getting sick. The vet examined him and said he had all the signs of pancreatitis. He wanted to admit Riley to the animal hospital for blood tests and hook him up to an IV drip. The cost was $1,450. It seemed a little extreme to me. Considering my cat's age, I declined the treatment and relied on home remedies. If Riley was going to die, I wanted him to be home. I put him on a raw diet and ensured he was well-hydrated. Within three days, he seemed to be better, but I knew it was only a matter of time until he had another attack. He depended on me, and I didn't want to let him down.

Guilt-ridden about leaving him again, I gave Riley more attention.

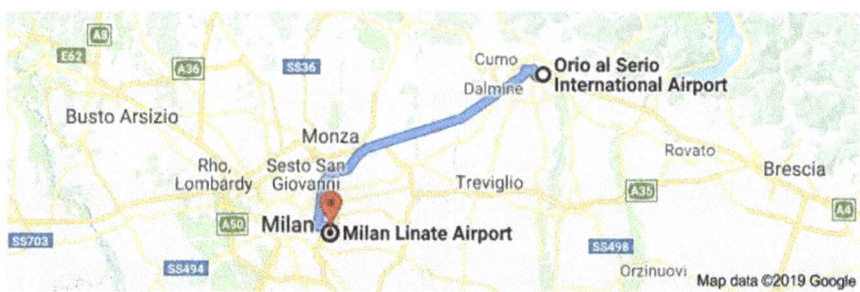

My ticket was confirmed for Sicily. This time, it wasn't a direct flight. I had to fly into Milan first and then take a connecting flight to Palermo. On top of that, my plane didn't land until after the last bus left for Sciacca. I'd have to find a hotel near the bus station.

The plane was at full capacity, not like the last time when I had an empty seat next to me. I had to sleep sitting up, but what concerned me more was the man next to me. He was sniffling and sneezing from the moment he sat down. I didn't want to get sick, so I turned in the opposite direction to breathe and put the extra blanket over my head.

Eventually, I dozed off. Surprisingly, I slept more than on the last flight. But when I awoke, my body ached. When I exited the plane in Milan to find my connecting flight to Palermo, an agent was at the gate. I calmly approached her for directions. She looked at my ticket and frowned.

"This connecting flight is at a different airport!"

"Oh. Where is the shuttle?" I asked.

"There is no shuttle," she replied. "You've arrived at the international airport. You must retrieve your luggage and take a taxi to the domestic airport to go to Palermo."

I felt the blood chill in my body, and my heart began to pump faster as my brain struggled to make sense of the situation. The airline had just dumped me in Milan, and I had to find my way to the connecting airport. I hoped I had adequate Italian to help me communicate. *Baby steps*, I thought, and held onto my composure by a fragile thread. A lovely couple standing next to me in line to go through customs and security suggested I take a bus. I had enough time, based on my layover time. *Okay*, I thought. I'm up for an adventure. When my suitcase came down the conveyor belt, I grabbed it and approached the information desk.

"Take bus number 2 out of Gate 4," the attendant said. "It will take you to that airport."

Of course, Gate 4 was at the end of the terminal. I dragged my suitcase at a quick pace and tried to look like I knew where I was going. When I arrived at bus 2, the driver said, "No! *Questo è l'autobus sbagliato*," and told me to try bus 5.

I ran down to the stop where a bus was already loading. Just as the door closed, I got the attention of the driver.

"*No! Questo non è l'autobus*," he said and directed me back to bus 2."

I had to communicate with *that* first driver again, who didn't know much English. Luckily, a nice Iranian man overheard my dilemma and stepped in to help. He told me I had to get off at the Central Station and transfer to another bus. I paid for my ticket and made sure to sit next to him.

We discussed politics and the fate of young people who don't value traditions today. Ali helped distract me from my travel anxiety. We arrived at the station, and then he was gone.

There were so many buses. I didn't know which one I had to take. Dragging my suitcase, I ran from bus to bus until I found the right bus, but I was sweating profusely and feeling sick. I had just missed it and had to wait another half an hour for the next one.

Traffic was heavy in Milan. *Will I make it in time for the flight to Palermo?* The city streets felt old and gray, weighed down by the overcast sky. I wondered why it was a popular destination.

I had to go through security again at the second Milan airport, which took longer. I made it to the gate with only a few minutes to spare. Exhausted, I plopped down in a seat and looked at my reservation paperwork. It was the same itinerary for my flight home. I called the travel agency to change my reservation on my return flight.

"You must complete your journey to Palermo first," the representative informed me.

As I waited to board the plane, I contemplated a nice cappuccino but noticed that the woman next to me was drinking a glass of wine. *Where did the morning go?* It was only three PM. Back in the U.S., my daughter sent me a text. Riley is doing great. He's eating and pooping every day."

Hmm. Is my daughter just saying that? Or maybe I have Munchausen-by-proxy syndrome.

Palermo Centrale

Lost Baggage

When the flight ended in Palermo, I felt more adventurous and opted to try the bus instead of taking a taxi. I found the correct number, loaded my suitcase, climbed aboard, and asked the driver which bus stop I should get off at for my hotel. He didn't speak English. Once again, a fellow passenger stepped in to help. She was a stylish woman from Milan who spoke excellent English. She asked the driver and determined I had to take the bus to Palermo Centre and then get off at Bus 305, which would take me to my hotel.

When the bus came to her stop, I thanked the woman again. I was alone. The driver let me know the next stop was mine, so I moved to the front of the bus. No one else was getting off, and no passengers were waiting to get on.

As I exited, I thought the driver was behind me to retrieve my suitcase under the bus, but the doors slammed shut, and he drove off. With my luggage!

Oh, no! "Wait!" I shouted and tried to chase the bus, but it was useless. He kept going. My calm demeanor evaporated, and I unspooled.

My heart raced as I realized everything I owned was inside that bag—my clothes, gifts, and phone charger—not to mention my cousin's European outlet adapter.

"Don't lose it," my cousin warned when I had asked to borrow it.

The only identifying information on the bag was the baggage claim from the airport. I couldn't catch my breath. *How was I going to get it? Should I take a cab to my hotel and ask for help, or return to the airport?*

A young man saw my anxiety, and he tried to help. We found the number of the bus company, and he offered to call them for me. I composed myself and succeeded until he told me the company had closed for the day! He suggested I remain at the stop and wait for my original bus to return.

My phone was dying, which made me panic even more. I pictured myself in the middle of the street with no way to communicate with anyone.

Just then, the hotel called. I explained my dilemma to the clerk, who spoke very little English. As I repeated myself, the original bus passed across the street. I didn't see it until it was too late. My frustration was apparent to the clerk at the hotel, but he apologized and said there was nothing he could do to help me.

The only hope was that another bus would pass along the same route. Within twenty minutes, I saw it approaching. Excited and relieved, I tried to wave it down, but to my dismay, the driver kept going! I wasn't under the sign for the bus stop, so he didn't see me.

As I tried to chase the bus, two Somali men approached me. They spoke a little English and suggested I go to the train station where all the buses stop. They offered to take me there, but I felt a little nervous and told them it wouldn't be wise to leave the bus stop. They seemed kind enough, but I didn't know them. Realizing my fear, they told me to take the next bus to the train station. "That one," they yelled as it approached the stop. They spoke to the bus driver in Italian, and he smiled.

"Non è un problema," he said, and I climbed aboard.

I didn't get to thank the two men who helped me in all the excitement, but I was grateful for their help. The station was about ten blocks away. As we approached, I saw my original bus.

"That's it," I said. "Stop!"

He shook his head. "Non una fermata!"

I had to get off at the next designated stop and then hurried to the corner, praying that the bus was still there. Between sobs, I poured out my story once more.

"Yes," the ticket attendant said. "Hanno trovato la tua valigia." They had found my suitcase. Seemingly unaffected, he called the depot and arranged for someone to bring it to the station.

"Lo porteranno qui. Aspettare!" He pointed away from the bus, directing me to wait by the building until they delivered it.

A few years ago, I looked much younger, and men were more eager to help me, but all they saw was an old lady. On the other side of youth, I couldn't go back. I felt insignificant, but I had to accept my fate.

I felt drained. I hadn't eaten anything all day, and my body hurt. I crossed the street and bought something to eat. I don't know what it was, some kind of pizza roll like the ones you'd find in the supermarket's freezer section, but my hunger got the best of me, and I scarfed it down without caring. A glass of wine made it more palatable.

Finally, my bag arrived, and the ticket attendant told me which bus to take, but I decided not to take any more chances. I had already lost three hours of daylight and wanted to get to my hotel, so I crossed the street and climbed into the first taxi I saw. At that point, my adventurous spirit faded.

It was a wise move because my hotel was outside the city limits. As we wound our way up the twisting road, the views of the city below got farther away. I wondered how I was going to get back in the morning.

Via Ruffo di Calabria

After a horrendous travel day, I was rewarded with the beautiful Hotel Bel 3, situated on top of a hill, clean and modern, with a bar and a restaurant. I was sorry I hadn't waited for dinner. The pizza roll I ate was resting uneasily in my stomach. The clerk gave me a knowing smile. "I'm happy that you found your baggage," he said. "A nice hot tub on the roof overlooks the city. You should go and relax."

    I would have done just that if I had gotten there earlier, but I was exhausted. After walking around the hotel and taking pictures, I went to my room and took a long, hot shower. Then I tried to sleep, but the time change wreaked havoc on my internal clock. Even with the P.M. pain reliever, I just tossed and turned. People downstairs were laughing and talking. Alone in my room wasn't how I wanted my day to end. So, I jumped up and dressed again. It didn't matter that I was tired. I followed the voices to the restaurant.

The restaurant was crowded. I felt the gaze of the other diners turn my way as the waiter seated me and cleared off the extra place settings. Why do restaurants always do that? If they had left the settings, at least it might have looked like I was expecting someone. Instead, their actions drew more attention to the table. I swallowed my aloneness and focused on the kitty that was allowed to scavenge food from people's plates. *Ha!*

You'd probably never see that in the States. It was refreshing to know that there were still places in the world that didn't adhere to stringent etiquette policies.

Since it was only four p.m. back home, I texted my cousin. At least I didn't have to tell her I had lost her converter. We corresponded until the waiter arrived with my dish, a large plate of pasta and salmon. It was so good. I finished it all and drank an entire carafe of red wine. I knew that fish went better with white wine, but I preferred red. Feeling full and content, I went back to my room and slept like a baby.

View of Palermo from the Hotel

Cine Campidoglio Multisala

Amore

In the morning, jet lag released me from its grip, and I called the airline to deal with the itinerary from hell. I insisted they change my flight, which they were all too happy to do—at an additional cost of $600! They said my travel insurance might cover it since it was considered a medical issue. But I suspected that, in the end, the company would find a reason not to honor it. There's always a loophole. Still, the airline representative gave me their telephone number and policy information, but they were closed on weekends. At this point, it didn't matter. I vowed never to try to save money on a flight to a different country, as it always cost more than I saved.

The bus to Sciacca was at eleven o'clock. This time, I took a taxi after the hotel shuttle dropped me off in town. Good move—even though it was within walking distance to the central bus station, had I listened to the clerk at the hotel, I would have missed the bus.

The ride to Sciacca was more pleasant than the last time, maybe because I knew what to expect and where to get off. Josie wasn't there to greet me, but I understood. She had just given birth to her daughter, Gloria. I didn't want to impose. Besides, I knew where I was going, and it wasn't too far.

Before I left the States, I checked the weather. It said the seventies, dipping to the fifties at night, but Sciacca felt as warm as Florida. I'd packed all wrong. Because Sicily is a small island, the climate changes quickly. A constant chill filled the air without the sun, but soon, the clouds moved off, and I ripped off my sweater as the temperature climbed.

I'd have to go shopping! Once I checked into Fazio's, I tried to message Josie. I looked forward to seeing her, but they only had one car, and Giovanni took it to work. She suggested we could get together for dinner on Friday if Giovanni wasn't too tired after work. Even though I was a little disappointed, I understood. Panic wanted to take over. What if I end up alone on this trip? After getting a grip, I reasoned, it wouldn't be so bad. Cousin Rita was coming with her sister Pina at the end of the week.

Since it was Sunday, all the stores were closed, including the restaurants, but I found one open for sports car racing fans. Their eyes were glued to the big screen as cars ripped around the tracks. I was looking forward to a pizza and a glass of wine, but the waitress informed me there was no pizza, only entrees. At least the menu was in both Italian and English. Unsure what to order, I ordered a pasta dish with eggplant and sausage. It wasn't until she left that I noticed the couple in front of me. The smell of their food grabbed me. I saw plates of delicious seafood, mussels, clams, squid, and fresh fish. I wish that I had seen it sooner. Though every table had a Coke bottle at the center, I ordered a small carafe of wine. It was anything but small. After drinking half the wine and eating one-quarter of my pasta dish, I asked for a takeaway. "No, problemo," the waitress said. She boxed up my meal and poured my wine into a plastic bottle. Yet, another thing you'd probably never see in the States.

I dropped the food back in my room, thinking dinner was in the bag, and walked to the supermercato, which seemed to be the only store open. While I was deciding which cheap wine to buy, an Italian man walked up to me. I kept telling him I didn't speak Italian, but he kept talking. I thought I had left him behind, but he pulled up to me in the parking lot after leaving the market and rolled down the window. Using sign language, he offered me a ride. I pretended that I didn't understand. "*Non-Capisco!*" I said, but he followed me as I walked through the streets. Luckily, I lost him once I crossed the bridge and came to the steps. I returned to the hotel for a long nap to ease my jet lag.

When I woke up, I dressed to walk to the piazza. The town seemed to come alive. There were people everywhere. The stores reopened, and music poured from the restaurants and cafés along the street. People crowded the streets, and children played in the piazza. It was still warm enough that I didn't need a sweater. I breathed in the sultry air, and my steps had a bounce.

I noticed a good-looking man in his early fifties standing by himself. I felt his eyes on me and smiled. Maybe I hadn't lost it yet.

I moved on and poked my head inside the Basilica to listen to the priest delivering the evening mass. The people sitting in the pews fanned themselves to relieve the heat since there was no air conditioning. I remained in the doorway for a while, then left.

Determined to buy something fit for summer, I entered a clothing store. Alas, after two spins around the shop, I realized the merchandise was intended for those under twenty-five. I moved on to the next shop, catering to older women. On top of that, the fabrics were heavy in anticipation of fall and winter. It didn't look like I'd find anything, so I continued to walk around.

A crowd had assembled down a small side street, so I went to investigate. I had found the local cinema, which was most likely playing films in Italian, but I put it on my mental list of things to do if it rained.

As I crossed the piazza again, I noticed the same man from before watching me. Feeling brave, I lingered a little longer and pretended to read a placard on the building before me. It worked. He approached me and began talking in Italian. The only thing I understood was his name. Michele.

"Non-Capisco," I said, and he pulled out his phone translator. I did the same. We stood in the center of the piazza, speaking through our phones, until he asked if I'd join him for a drink.

"Si," I heard myself say, and we walked along the narrow street to find a place. I excused myself to wash my hands in the bathroom while he ordered a bottle of wine and two large plates of meats and cheeses. I wouldn't have leftover pasta and eggplant for dinner after all!

We sat and translated until his battery died, and mine got low. We drank most of the wine. I thought he might take the leftovers, but he waved them off. I let him walk me back to my hotel and promised to see him again the next day. As we walked through the streets, my hand brushed against his, and he clasped it. Holding hands felt very romantic, but I didn't intend to let him come to my room. Using the last bit of energy from my phone, I told him I had a lovely evening and hoped to get to know him better. He hugged me close and tried to kiss me on the lips. I turned my head, and the kiss landed on my cheek. He smiled and stood back as I unlocked the door, waiting until I stepped safely inside. Safely inside, I peeked out to see him walking away. What a wonderful evening, I thought. I wasn't sure if he was right for me, but I'd always been so scared to let anyone in, and sometimes I regretted passing up opportunities.

The way I figured it, at my age, finding love was like musical chairs. If you hesitate, you lose your seat.

Piazza Girolamo Lombardo

Bocce Ball

I woke up feeling refreshed and ready to tackle my travel housekeeping. Thank goodness I bought the travel insurance. Having a panic attack at an unfamiliar airport seemed like a medical issue for me. I called the company, but they were closed. I left a message and contacted the hotel booking agency to say I needed to change my hotel reservation. Since I changed my flight, I stayed in Sicily for two extra days. The agency informed me they couldn't change the itinerary but promised to inquire at the hotel. Their concern didn't give me hope, though. I've learned from experience that companies like that know how to soften the blow. It's part of their job to unruffle feathers.

I searched for another room. I'd been there before and knew I'd survive my bruised ego and wallet. This trip had already cost me double, but being in a foreign country, I had to accept it as a costly learning experience.

On my way out to explore the town, I asked the staff at the front desk to check airport transportation on the weekends, but the bus didn't run on Sunday, so I had to leave a day sooner and stay in Palermo again.

Although there was a pleasant breeze outside, the temperature was higher than expected. Jeans were not going to be an option during the day. I found a small Asian shop with inexpensive clothing on my last trip and purchased summer clothes. As I navigated over the bridge, I kept an eye out for the man I met at the supermercato the previous day. He insisted I take his number, but I didn't plan to call him.

The streets were empty. I had forgotten that Sciacca shops closed between one and five o'clock every day. With shopping on hold, I went for a stroll to the park. Along the way, I passed the piazza, where an old man was playing the flute. His audience was a group of workers below him. They seemed to enjoy the entertainment as much as I did. Once I had my fill, I continued my walk.

From behind me, I heard my name called out. Did I imagine it?

Oh no! It was the man from the supermercato. He wore a bright yellow shirt and pants and reminded me of Big Bird from Sesame Street. I had to get rid of him somehow. I continually repeated, "Non-Capisco," but he kept talking. I said it loud enough so the people around us knew he was unwelcome, but no one seemed to care. They just walked on like they do in New York City.

Finally, I told him mi dispiace and walked off. I wasn't really sorry. I just wanted to go for a peaceful walk by myself.

Hoping to catch some locals playing a bocce ball game, I went to the park.

Bocce is a form of bowling made famous by the Romans. The object is to get your bocce ball closest to the target. Each player rolls or tosses the small ball underhand down a dirt lane.

There was a bocce ball game going on. I stopped to watch for a while and sat down on a bench. One of the older men came and sat next to me and asked if I was a *turista*. I didn't need a translator to decipher his words, but I pulled out my phone to show that my grandfather was born in Sciacca. Does that make me a tourist? I'd like to think not, but I'm sure they'd disagree.

It was a warm, sunny day, so I walked to the beach. Mostly, you find small stones like prehistoric eggs in beautiful patterns and colors. Shells are rare on the Sciacca shores.

The temperature was in the low 80s, but no one was in the water. I took the long way back to the piazza, wary that "Big Bird" would still be lurking around.

Basilica Madonna del Soccorso

I walked to the marina again as the sun dipped lower in the sky. In the distance, I saw the steeple of a church down at the port. It wasn't as big as the Basilica but had a unique design and looked older. Inside, a mass was in session. I had always attended church on Sunday mornings but never at night. The excessive heat didn't lessen the congregation—the church was packed. That was true devotion.

On the way back to my hotel, I took a side street and stumbled upon another shopping district filled with restaurants. One, in particular, caught my eye. Osteria Cappellino was tucked away in a small historic alley. Outside, colorful umbrellas hung upside down from strings above.

Osteria Cappellino – Via Cappellino

Dirty Bird

Michele wanted to see me again after he finished work for dinner. I told him I'd meet him outside at six pm. He came down the street on time as I exited my hotel. I thought it was odd that he was wearing the same clothes from the day before.

After a brief hug, he translated that we were going to a unique restaurant for dinner. To my surprise, it was the same one with umbrellas overhead.

Unfortunately, the seating was full. "Maybe another restaurant," Michele translated, but I wanted to eat in that one, so I suggested walking around for a while. It was a beautiful night.

Sure enough, my wish came true. We were seated under the umbrellas, and Michele ordered us some wine.

We were getting the hang of the phone app, which translated whoever was talking into Italian or English.

"Troppo cibo," I said, seeing all that food. Michele laughed and suggested I fast the next day. The first dish arrived at our table. Little fried fish with the heads still on.

"Are these sardines?" I asked.

"No," he said. "Questo è bluefish."

Hesitantly, I bit the head off one. It was crunchy and quite tasty. Still, the thought of the fish's head on my tongue made me queasy. The dishes kept coming, and I remained adventurous in trying everything. My mind returned to when I visited my Chinese friend, Virginia, in New York. At my request, she whispered our order to the waitress. I didn't want to know what I was eating until after the fact. It turned out to be tuna belly, raw eel, and cow tongue. Ugh! The tongue kept me up all night, not because of the taste but the texture. When I thought my stomach couldn't hold any more food, the main dish arrived. I moaned as I looked at the giant prawn, grilled squid, and large tuna filet. By the time we finished the wine, I had thought they'd have to roll me out.

We smiled and translated all through the four courses of dinner. Michele paid the check, and we walked hand in hand to the marina. It was a beautiful, balmy night, and I felt comfortable with him.

"Ti voglio bene," he said.

I laughed nervously. "Non è possibile!"

We gazed out at the Mediterranean from the piazza, and he slipped his arm around my shoulder. As he drew closer, his hands began to wander, and I stiffened with discomfort. The stale scent of two-day-old clothes clung to him, hitting my nostrils as he leaned in. Before I could react, he was smothering me with kisses. Then came the question—could he come up to my room?

I translated that I had only known him for two days.

Dirty bird, I thought. Thinking on my feet, which is much better than lying down, I translated that it was too soon and we should take one day at a time.

Michele argued that we had little time because I was only there for five more days. "I think you may be Pinocchio," he said in Italian, but even without translating, I realized his brewing anger.

Something clicked, and I panicked. I wasn't trying to be dishonest. I truly wanted to have a romantic experience, but when I saw the red flags, any warm and fuzzy feeling I had for Michele quickly dissipated. I had to cut him loose.

Like my cat, Riley, he wouldn't take no for an answer. No matter how many times I pushed him off my lap, he tried to climb back up until I gave in and petted him. At least Riley didn't get mad. I sensed that Michele had an Italian temper. Because I never liked confrontation, I always had difficulty saying no to people in English. How was I supposed to break up with him in Italian?

Somehow, I convinced him we'd see each other again before I left. He tried to kiss me goodbye, but before he groped me again, I pulled away and said, "Domani."

The promise of seeing him the next day was enough to set me free, and I quickly entered the protection of my hotel. *How did I get myself into this mess?* There wasn't enough hot water to wash away his scent and my foolishness.

Pani e Panelle

By morning, I had a plan. First, I texted Michele and told him that I was sick. "Too much food, too much wine, and too much emotion," I said. I thought that was that, but he wasn't about to give up too quickly. I couldn't get that stupid song out of my head… "I've got no strings to hold me down." I imagined the Sicilian headlines in the morning paper… *American woman killed due to an act of passion.*

    My daughter called to assure me that Riley was doing well. She even said he didn't miss me at all. I didn't know what to think of that! Maybe she was trying to reassure me, and it was true. I felt relieved he was doing fine, but I didn't need to know he didn't miss me. *Geez!* American children don't seem to consider their parents' feelings the way Italians do.

I didn't want to spend the day alone and thought about my cousin Rita. We must have been on the same track because my phone chimed with an incoming message. "I'm so sorry I haven't contacted you sooner. My phone isn't working in Italy, so I'm using my sister's. Do you want to meet me for lunch?" We agreed to meet at 11:30 in front of the church. I ducked into the breakfast room for a cup of cappuccino and wrapped a pistachio croissant in a napkin to save for a midnight snack.

Since it was early, there was a gentle breeze. I stopped in a store to browse, stood in the shade across from the Basilica, and waited. Twenty minutes later, no Rita. I sent a text to her sister.

"She should have been there already," Pina said.

Oh, no, I thought. Perhaps Rita had gone to a different church.

I remembered another church was up the block from my hotel. I hurried back through the piazza and narrow streets. When I got to the church, there was no sign of Rita. Circling back, I took a different road back to the Basilica. No Rita. I texted her sister again and asked for their address, figuring she might have given up and gone home. I wish that I had worn shorts. The temperature was climbing, and the breeze had stopped.

Before taking the journey, I went back to my hotel to change. I heard someone ringing the front bell as I was preparing to leave. The staff often disappeared, so if someone without a key wanted to come in, they had to ring. I wondered if it was Rita. Flying down the stairs, I looked outside to see her beautiful face, stressed and overheated as much as mine. We exchanged a hot, sticky hug.

"I'm starving," she said.

"So am I. Where should we eat?"

"I have to have *pani e panelle*," she insisted.

"What's that?"

"You'll see. They're delicious."

We walked past the Basilica down to the park to a food truck. I'd often passed that truck when walking, but I thought it was fast food. Shows what I knew. Rita was born in Sciacca and said *pani e panelle* was the first thing she wanted to eat whenever she visited. She ordered two big sandwiches and a side of rice balls.

"So much food," I said. "We're going to be fat."

"Nonsense. We'll walk it off."

The delicately fried pillows containing chickpeas were as good as Rita promised. She finished the whole sandwich, while I only ate half of mine, plus one rice ball. We spent the day walking, laughing, talking, and enjoying each other's company.

Via Perollo

Family Homestead

I had walked through Sciacca at least ten times since my first visit and passed a sloped street that led to houses. Little did I know it was where my grandfather had grown up. Rita led me to the area where some of our family still lived. She said we had many cousins in the neighborhood. We arrived at a small courtyard, and she showed me the house where her Nonna grew up and later raised her family of nine children. It was hard to believe so many people had fit into such a small space.

Cortile Chiodi

Most of Nonna's children stayed in Sciacca. Rita recalled that her grandmother cried all the time when her sister, Anna, and her brother, Giuseppe, left for the States because she didn't think she'd ever see them again. It was expensive to make international calls, and there were no computers or email. They had to rely on letters, which became less frequent as the pressure of raising a family took over.

If there had been any letters, my mother never mentioned them. They were probably read and discarded.

Behind the Commune, we entered a large courtyard. The placard outside read, "Ex Collegio dei Gesuiti," and Rita told me that once, it housed orphans and children temporarily placed there because their parents couldn't care for them.

Ex Collegio dei Gesuiti

During World War II, times were tough, and many men had to leave the town to serve in the Italian Army. Their wives had to provide for the children. Two of those children were Rita's sisters, Pina and Maria. I tried to imagine what it was like for them. "They weren't alone," Rita said, "because many of our cousins lived there, too."

At the edge of town, our family lived and thrived in the fishing industry by the sea. The Corraos and Ruffos reportedly owned almost ninety percent of the fishing fleet, as most of the men in our family were fishermen. Sometimes, they'd go out to sea for months, leaving their wives dressed in black until they returned as a sign of worry and tradition. We walked along the shoreline to the house where Rita's family lived, and she painted verbal pictures for me of her childhood.

I imagined the shrimping fleet moving out before sunrise and their return at the end of the day, teeming with the briny smell of fresh fish. Rita used to help sort the shrimp. She wore rubber gloves and an oversized apron to scoop up the shrimp and put them in containers. She needed to stand on a platform to reach them. I pictured her little arms reaching into the barrel.

We had the nerve to knock on the door of her childhood home. A man answered and said he remembered the family. He let us come inside and look around. It was very nostalgic for Rita, whose mother had passed away recently. We looked down at the sea from the balcony, and she recalled the times she and her siblings climbed down the hill to swim.

The simplicity of life was astounding. I wondered if my grandfather did the same thing.

On the Coast off the Rock of Regina

Rock of Regina

Rita took me to the Rock of Regina, a special place where a beautiful mermaid watched over the sea and sang to guide the fishermen back home. Some still claimed to hear her soft, sweet voice floating on the wind.

    She told me about the legend of Maria Santissima del Soccorso. I had heard of the patron saint of Sciacca, Our Lady of Distress, but I didn't know how she ended up in the Basilica. In the 1600s, some fishermen went out to make a catch. They cast their nets every day, but the sea gave them nothing. After a week, the fishermen became desperate. Still no fish. They prayed to the Virgin Mary and cast their nets out again.

Miraculously, as they pulled in the nets, it surfaced with a multitude of fish. The weight required four men to hoist it onto the ship's deck. Among the fish, there was a statue. It was the Madonna. Their prayers were answered. The statue was restored and enshrined in the main church. Twice a year, Maria Santissima del Soccorso is paraded through the streets of Sciacca and taken to the sea to bless it. Only the fishermen were allowed to carry her.

We passed a bar as we made our way through the side streets. It was called Bar Charlie. My cousin Jason mentioned it in an email. He said a distant family member owned it. Rita knew who it was, a relative on her father's side of the family, but he wasn't there.

Following the Mediterranean shore, we came to her mother's house. Giuseppa, or Pina, as she was called, was waiting for us. She was just as delightful as Rita.

The family connection deepened when their sister, Maria, arrived. I was surprised that she had blonde hair, but my family's resemblance was evident, although she was more reserved. Out of four sisters, she was the only one who had remained in Sicily. Pina lived in Boston, and Brigida resided in New Jersey. I met her at our cousin's reunion. They had a brother, Calogero, who lived in Brooklyn, and another, Vincenzo, who lived on Staten Island.

Via Lido

Maria, Pina, Rita, and I sat around their mother's table, drinking coffee and looking at the passing boats. They were my family, yet less than a year ago, I didn't know they existed. We made plans to visit the cemetery. I almost had to pinch myself. I was in this beautiful home overlooking the Mediterranean. My cousins wanted to see their mother's grave, which might give us a chance to find our great-grandparents' graves. Cousin Maria warned that they might not be there because in Sicily, bones are often exhumed after a few years and moved elsewhere.

The Shores of the Mediterranean

La Famiglia Salvatore Ruffo
(Cousin Rita's Family)

Cimitero

In Sciacca, flyers displayed on walls and the sides of buildings announced the passing of someone in the community. It is typical to see an obituary in the local newspaper when someone dies in America. In recent years, there has been a growing trend to memorialize the place where someone has lost their life due to a fatal car accident. You will see these roadside memorials on the highways and along suburban streets. They serve two purposes. It is a way for families to honor their loved ones and warn other drivers to slow down and drive cautiously. Typically, the spot is marked by a cross and flowers. It was always sad to see a stuffed animal, letting you know it was a child who had lost their life, especially after the toys were exposed to the elements — sun and rain.

I was surprised at how close the cemetery was to my hotel. It was only a twenty-minute walk. There was a flower stand outside the cemetery gates. Most of the visitors stopped and bought bouquets to put on the graves. The flowers were held upside down, and I asked Rita about it. She said it was because the flowers were for the dead, not the living. They weren't meant for *our* enjoyment.

After lovingly placing flowers on their mother's grave, Pina and Maria had to take care of the paperwork for their mother's will at the courthouse and left us to explore.

We found the gravesite of Nonna Maria, her grandmother and my great-aunt, but we couldn't find our great-grandfather, Paolo, and great-grandmother, Maria, in a sea of graves.

We noticed a young man working in the front office as we were leaving the cemetery. Rita spoke to him in Italian, and he agreed to search the record books for our grandparents. We told him we'd be back the next day.

Corrao Family Tomb

Corrao Fratelli

Rita had wanted to introduce me to another cousin, Maria, but her son had married the night before, and she didn't answer her phone. I was a little disappointed, but I understood. We returned to the cemetery to see if the clerk had found information on our great-grandparents. As we entered the cemetery gates, someone called out Rita's name. The woman ran over, and they hugged. Their conversation was in Italian, so I had no idea what they were saying until Rita turned to me. "This is your cousin Maria!" she said. "The one I wanted you to meet."

"Really?" I couldn't believe it. What were the chances? Living in a small town, you were bound to run into people.

Maria stared at my face. "She looks like Nonna," she said in Italian. We hugged and took a few pictures together. Since she was with guests from out of town, she had to leave, but she made me promise to come back to Sciacca for a visit. For sure, I had to learn Italian.

The man in the front office noticed us coming. He ran out to tell us he had found the family mausoleum and led us to a tall building. It said, "CORRAO FRATELLI."

A single rose propped in the handle signified that there had been a recent visitor. We peeked in the window, amazed at the tomb that lined each side. At the back of the tomb was a white altar. A picture hung on the wall. I wondered if it was my great-great-great Grandfather Pasquale Corrao, and his wife, Rosa Dieciedue, but there was no name. More likely, his grandson, Pasquale, was born in 1851. We didn't see our great-grandfather Paolo's name, so we kept searching the cemetery.

As we left the mausoleum and came across a section dedicated to sailors and fishermen, we saw a scaffold piled with bricks and a bucket of mortar. Four attendants carried a casket and slid it into the opening. The mourners watched as a worker stacked the blocks until the coffin was concealed behind them. The man cemented over them, so it was a solid wall, and scribbled the deceased's name with his finger. Finally, he fixed a picture in the upper right-hand corner. I had hoped to watch them place the marble slab in front, but they didn't as the mortar had to dry. Once he was done, he meticulously cleaned the stones surrounding the opening, then brushed and swept every bit of dust off the other gravestones. There were so many graves! We tried to find the family name. Our search wasn't successful, and it was getting late.

Pizza Mia

Josie and her family came to pick me up for dinner. They pulled up in separate cars at the end of my road. Cars in Europe are generally smaller. Partly because they're economical and because parking is a premium commodity.

I climbed into the back seat with Josie's father, Carlo, at the wheel. He and his wife spoke English, so the pressure was off. They understood everything I said. Incredibly, Josie's father turned out to be Rita's cousin, which made us related through marriage. The first time I visited Sciacca, I thought maybe Josie's husband was my cousin because his mom's name was

Maria Corrao. He insisted we weren't related, but his mother looked exactly like my cousin Linda back in the States.

Rita laughed and said, "Everyone in the town is related at some point."

La Grande Valle Pizzeria was up in the hills near San Calogero. And grand it was! I had dreamed about their delicious pizza since my last visit. Last time, I only ate half because I was still full from lunch, but this time, I planned to eat it all, including the yummy olive they put in the center. I asked Josie why they did that, but she wasn't sure.

I thought about the little plastic piece that some pizzerias used. Maybe it's so the pizza doesn't get squished. If that's true, it's genius.

Whatever the reason, it was a nice touch, and I wondered why no one in the States ever thought of doing it. Perhaps they didn't want the added expense, but if I ever had owned a pizzeria, I'd make sure there was a plump, juicy olive in the middle of every pie.

At the end of the night, I kissed Josie and her family goodbye, wondering if I'd ever see them again.

Piazza Girolamo Lombardo

Armenian Detour

I arrived one hour before my bus was due to leave the station. It was enough time to get another treat from the street vendors. Instead of Pani e Panelle, I bought a cone of fried calamari. Unlike the States, they didn't use tomato sauce, just a little salt, pepper, and a squeeze of lemon. I sat on a bench in the park and ate my lunch. A large stone inscribed with the Italian words, *A Tutti I Caduti Contro La Mafia,* sat in the middle of the park. Curious, I googled the phrase. The English translation said, "All the Fallen Against the Mafia."

Sadly, I loaded my suitcase into the luggage compartment beneath the bus when it arrived, a little hesitant but more aware than the last time. I found a comfortable seat near the window and sighed. I stared out my window and watched the landscape change as we left the city and rolled past orchards and farms. The *Autobus* twisted and turned through the streets, roads, and over hills and vineyards as it followed the lay of the land. Along the sides of the road, I noticed square holes in the ground, the size and shape of a swimming pool, and wondered if they were there to collect water.

After we pulled into Palermo city center, I was the first passenger waiting for my luggage. I reviewed the directions to my hotel and headed to the local bus depot on the other side of the station. Following the blue arrows, I passed the trains and some restaurants. I should have kept going, but I suddenly felt unsure. I spotted a clean-cut man wearing a business suit and carrying a briefcase. I assumed he was on his way home from the office, so I approached him and asked where the buses were. He looked at my directions and shook his head. He told me the bus depot was far away and suggested I cancel my reservation and find one closer to the city. He even offered to help me find one. I made a quick calculation and realized that, perhaps, he didn't have my best interests at heart. Something didn't seem right. I called my hotel and explained the situation. The receptionist asked to speak to him, and I put him on the phone. He seemed to be arguing with the girl and looked annoyed, then he handed me my phone and walked off.

The receptionist confirmed my suspicions. "Don't leave with this man," she said. "I'm sending a car for you."

If the clerk at my hotel hadn't intervened, I might have trusted the wrong person, too. Abductions are not always violent. Traffickers targeted tourists who were unfamiliar with the territory. They were easy prey.

After narrowly escaping what could have been a traumatic event, I checked into my hotel and thanked the clerk who came to my rescue. She mentioned that some recent migrant groups had been linked to criminal activity in the region.

According to Wikipedia, Armenia is a source country known for its sex trafficking gangs. Women are taken from the streets and from the airport and forced into slavery or prostitution. As dramatized in the fictional movie *Taken* with Liam Neeson, it is tough to track these criminals down. According to the U.S. State Department, human trafficking is a global problem on the rise.

Under pressure, the Armenian government increased the minimum penalty to five years imprisonment for convicted trafficking offenders.

The perpetrators moved their operations to Sicily and California, where they were considered the new Mafia. Local officials in Sicily were complacent, and the number of victims doubled in one year.

Bellevue del Golfo

My hotel in Palermo was in the seaside village of *Castellammare del Golfo*. It overlooked the fishing port, and I had a perfect view of the harbor. Boats of all sizes dotted the horizon. To my delight, I discovered there was a special event going on, and the town was dressed up for the annual Fisherman's Fall Festival.

The weight of the situation at the bus station lessened, and I wanted to feel the pulse of the town. Putting my fears aside, I ventured out from the safety of my hotel and walked toward the music and lights. Lost among the crowds of families, tourists, and children, I felt at ease and wandered through the tent-lined side streets.

Packed with festival celebrations, the restaurants had standing room only as groups waited to be seated. Since I was alone, getting a small table with a view of the sea wasn't hard. I sipped a glass of Rosso as the warm sea breeze caressed my cares away. I glanced down at the menu. There were so many dishes I wanted to try, but I was down to my last ten euros, and the only method of payment the restaurant accepted was cash. Luckily, the clams and linguine were within my budget. Since my specialty was clams in white sauce, I opted for red instead. I wasn't disappointed.

The following day, I took the hotel shuttle to the airport and said goodbye to Sicily.

The Last Corrao Daughter

The Christmas holiday wasn't merry. When my niece entered the bedroom on the morning of Christmas Eve, she found that my mother was in trouble. Although her eyes were wide open, she wasn't able to speak. An ambulance rushed her to the hospital. It turned out that her blood sugar was only thirty. They gave her insulin and took some tests. My mother's kidneys were failing. They released her because it was

Christmas Eve, but made us promise to bring her right after dinner.

My mother ate everything on her plate and enjoyed a beer at the restaurant. I never even knew she liked beer, but she felt so good, she had another. When it was time to bring her back to the hospital, we didn't want to take her, but my mother insisted. I wasn't sure what the right thing to do was, so I agreed she should return. It was a decision I have since gone over again and again in my mind.

The nurses pumped her with fluids and potassium. She blew up like a balloon, and the doctor admitted her to the hospital. My siblings and I sat by her hospital bed for almost a month. They poked and prodded her until her arms were black and blue. She wasn't in pain from her kidneys, but they were functioning at a low level. Since she wasn't a candidate for a kidney transplant, they just made her comfortable. The doctor suggested calling hospice to begin morphine treatment, but I didn't see the rush. She woke a few times a day and carried on a conversation. We wouldn't be able to communicate if they doped her up on drugs.

The nurses soon got tired of changing her bedding and ordered a Foley. She wanted to go home, but the only way they agreed to release her was if she agreed to receive hospice care at home. It was downhill from there. None of us truly understood what hospice care would mean or how close the end really was.

They set up a hospital bed in my mother's living room. A hospice nurse monitored her all day until another relieved her at night. At first, we fed her small quantities of soft food and dietary shakes, but as the morphine increased, her appetite decreased. Finally, the nurse told us not to feed her anymore because it just sat in her mouth. She couldn't swallow—no more tuna sandwiches, peanut butter on toast, meatballs, or hot dogs—strangely her favorite.

After a week with no food, my mother barely opened her eyes. We believed she could still hear us, but she was too weak to respond. I leaned in close and whispered in her ear. "I'm taking you with me to Sciacca this spring." I thought we both understood. It wouldn't be a physical journey but a spiritual one.

Although we expected her to pass, my family was shocked when she stopped breathing. They transported her to the funeral home with nothing more than the cross my brother put around her neck and a hospital gown. We anticipated a full funeral with a viewing and mass. We discovered she only had enough money in her life insurance policy to cremate her. I knew she wanted to be buried beside her dear sister, Anna Lucy. My brother came through with additional money to fulfill her wishes.

The funeral parlor had my beloved mother transported to the cemetery in a plain white van. She was laid to rest in a basic coffin covered in blue felt with only the cross around her neck. I didn't get to view her, but the memory of her life fading as she lay in her living room was disturbing enough. She was the last daughter of Giuseppe Corrao. Her older sister Mary had passed away a year before. I insisted that her photo be etched into the gravestone like in Sicily.

There is something about losing your mother that hurts your heart's very deepest parts.

My mother always wanted to become a famous singer and make her father proud. Unfortunately, she never fulfilled her dream. After recording two records, she married my father, and the babies started coming.

I took solace in knowing she wasn't suffering anymore, but now, my pain had to be endured. Trying to stay busy, I went on with the process of living, with sudden waves of depression that kept trying to surface.

I picked up my phone for weeks and began dialing her number, only to realize she would no longer be there to answer. She was always there for me whenever I called, sometimes two or three times a day. It was harder to communicate after her stroke, but the sound of her voice was a comfort. I searched for her old voicemail messages, but was disappointed to find I'd erased them.

Before I knew it, I was on my way back to Sicily. This time, I'd be going with Marie from the Puleo side of the family and her daughter, Marianna. Marie was my mother's cousin, which made her my second cousin. Her father, Joseph, was the only child of Anna Corrao. Joseph married Marianne, and they started a Christmas tree company, now world-renowned as Puleo International, Inc. They had four children: Anthony, Salvatore, Anita, and Marie.

Marie lived in Guatemala, where she and her two sons ran a family restaurant. Marianna grew up in Guatemala, later moved to Manhattan, and now speaks multiple languages fluently, including Italian.

La Famiglia Anna Corrao Puleo

Palermo

At least on my third trip to Sicily, I wouldn't be the only one who couldn't speak Italian. After Easter, my first cousins, Billy and Jane, joined us. Their mother, Mary, had passed away one year before my mother, the last of the Corrao sisters. We planned to memorialize the four daughters of our grandfather, Giuseppe, in some small way.

    We'd be staying in Sicily for almost three weeks. I thought that should be enough time to learn about my family's roots and discover what happened to my great-grandparents, Paolo and Maria. We planned to pay a visit to the Comune. I had passed those official doors of city hall both times I was in Sciacca, but was too afraid to enter since I didn't speak Italian and couldn't communicate with the government workers.

I took a separate flight from Florida to JFK Airport and had a four-hour window before my trip to Sicily. First, I had a stopover in Atlanta, but I didn't think it was a problem because both flights were on Delta. But Marianna thought I was taking a risk.

I checked the Delta schedule online, and the flight to Atlanta was on time. The status had changed when I arrived at the airport, and the attendant announced a delay. I rushed up to the counter and told her about my connecting flight. She said I might not make my connection because I had to take the train to another terminal once I landed in Atlanta. She rescheduled me for the next flight with a three-hour layover. If the plane was on time, I'd have one hour to check in at the International Terminal. I began to panic. I asked the attendant to keep my seat open for the first flight if I made it on time. And that's just what I did. Running through the terminal, I made it with twenty minutes to spare, then sat back and waited for my cousins, relieved that I wouldn't have to face the embarrassment of their warnings.

The flight was uneventful—no babies and no sick passengers. Marie and her daughter, Marianna, sat together in a double seat, and I sat in the middle aisle. I was lucky to have an empty seat next to me and could get a few hours of sleep.

Well-rested, we disembarked in Rome to catch our second flight to Palermo. Although the airport was laid out in an organized way, with plenty of signs, the extra security of traveling with others made me calmer.

Marianna wasn't feeling well. She took some cold medicine, and by the time we reached our first B&B apartment, she said she felt better.

We ventured into the streets of Palermo and stopped for dinner at a restaurant. It had outdoor seating, and the sun felt good, but it didn't last long. Soon, the evening shadows grew longer, and the wind picked up.

Deterred by the chill in the air, we hit the supermarket across from our apartment for wine and morning yogurt and then returned to rest.

The next day, we left Palermo and made our way around Sicily. We stopped in small towns to let passengers on and off the bus. Our first stop was Trapani, a city northwest of Palermo, known for its Easter procession. As the bus hugged the coast, I had periodic views of the beautiful blue Tyrrhenian Sea on my right. Seaside vineyards dotted the landscape, along with tropical bushes bearing yellow flowers. On my left, the ruins of a long-forgotten past sprang up between farms, thriving in every shade of green.

Our apartment was on the top floor, and with no elevator, we had to brave the stairs with our suitcases. It felt colder inside than outside, but it had a full kitchen and internet.

Trapani | 153

Marianna wasn't feeling well, so Marie and I went for a morning walk to find coffee. Along with my cappuccino, I had a Pasticcottio—one of my favorites, but it wasn't a tart. This version was shaped like a pastry pocket.

Nine Digits

Marie told me the story of her grandfather, Salvatore Puleo. He and my great aunt Anna owned a fish market in Elizabeth, New Jersey. The Mafia ignored him until they saw that Salvatore was making good money. He had begun selling unusual vegetables he imported directly from Italy, and they wanted him to pay them protection money. Well, Salvatore wouldn't conform. No matter how they tried to strong-arm him, he refused to give them a dime. At three a.m., Salvatore Puleo kissed his wife and petted his dog before walking to the docks to buy his daily fish. It was a foggy morning, and he didn't see the two men coming up behind him. One grabbed him and shoved a blade into him. Salvatore Puleo wouldn't go down without a fight, and they scuffled. He clamped onto the guy's thumb with his teeth and bit it clean off. The thug, now missing a digit, cried out in pain while the other pulled out a gun and shot Salvatore.

Salvatore's dog began to bark back in the house and alerted his wife that something had happened. She looked outside the window and saw her husband on the ground, bleeding and barely alive. Miraculously, he survived seven stab wounds and nine gunshots. Salvatore had to look over his shoulder from then on, but the Mafia never bothered him again. The stories fascinated me. I wanted to hear more, but it was getting late. We had to go back to the apartment to check on Marianna.

Maria Grammatico's Bakery in Erice

Marzipan Lambs

Marianna insisted she was feeling better and wanted to go with us to see the Easter procession at the church. Although there was a bite in the air, the sun peeked out and warmed us. The Easter procession in Trapani had taken place on Wednesday — we missed it by two days — but we were on time for the fourteen Stations of the Cross scheduled for Good Friday. We watched the floats emerge from the church but didn't follow the procession. Instead, we toured the church, which depicted each Station of the Cross.

We moved on to Erice, a small city that overlooks Trapani. The only way up was by funicular, a railway car pulled on a slope by a cable. We were high above the city. It felt as if we were in the clouds. It was about twenty degrees colder at the top, and we huddled together as we climbed the steep pathways.

Marie told us about the famous baker Maria Grammatico. Her mother sent her to a convent when she was eleven because there was no money to feed Maria and her five siblings. In preparation to become a nun, she woke up at dawn each day and worked in the kitchen, making almond-based *pasticcini*, which the nuns sold to sustain themselves.

Fifteen years later, she decided to leave the convent, taking her baking skills with her. The nuns were displeased, and they made things difficult for Maria. She was persistent and baked at her house. She soon became famous for her Easter lambs made from marzipan. She opened a bakery at the top of Erice and wrote a book about her life. *Bitter Almonds.*

We were delighted to see an open sign in the window. To top it all off, we met Maria. I wanted to buy her book, which was selling in the shop, but it was only in Italian, so I looked it up on Amazon.

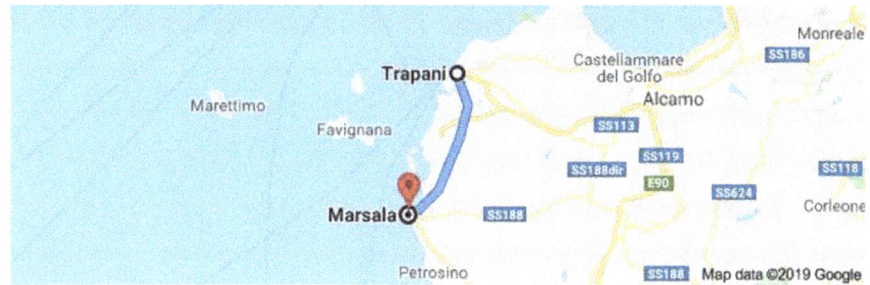

Marsala

The next town was Marsala, which had a flatter landscape than Trapani. Besides being famous for its wine, Marsala is known for its many open ponds. Conditions are ideal for salt production, as the sun and the wind slowly evaporate seawater and leave behind dry salt.

Every year, Marsala goes all out with its elaborate Easter procession. Actors dress up in costume and reenact the story of Jesus' crucifixion.

Royalty marched down the streets in long, flowing robes, their heads adorned with jewels, each carrying a staff. Men of the church followed in pious attire, and women dressed in mourning.

Roman gladiators rode beautiful horses with braided manes, and tunic-clad soldiers on foot cracked their whips to control prisoners in chains and push them forward. Some captives had their arms tied to large planks of wood and had difficulty holding them up as they moved along. Roman women wore colorful silk stolas with ribbons tied just below the bust to create an empire waist. In ancient Roman times, the wealthiest women had the most folds in their Pallae. They pulled them over their heads to protect themselves from inclement weather or maintain privacy.

Peasants dressed in a humbler garb of simple brown cloth wore headscarves, while the young maidens donned blue and white robes. The children were dressed in white tunics tied with a belt. They carried large palm leaves. One small boy cradled a live rooster, signifying the cock that crowed while Judas betrayed Jesus.

There were many versions of Jesus. One of the most impressive characterizations was Jesus in white robes, blessing the children and reciting prophecies. Another actor portraying Jesus, carrying the cross, was urged on by his captors' whip. Although it was a reenactment, it was deeply moving.

Afterward, we stopped for gelato. Marie and Marianna returned to the apartment to rest. I took to the streets to explore.

As the sun sank low in the sky, I followed the sounds of music coming from a small bar. Inside, a musical duo was performing. One played the guitar, and the other played the bongos. I ordered a glass of red wine and enjoyed the show.

The driver who was supposed to take us to the train station sent a message that he was unavailable, so we had to wake up before dawn and walk to the train station with our noisy suitcases rolling over the uneven cobblestone pavement. If we missed the train, we wouldn't have a way to get to Mazara del Vallo, where our cousin Santo planned to pick us up in the town square. It was a chilly morning, and it took thirty minutes to get there.

Legend has it that Arabian troops stormed the harbor and headed toward Syracuse. Mazara del Vallo is said to be one of the leading trade towns.

We made it with only minutes to spare and met up with Cousin Santo, one of Nonna Maria's grandchildren. He dropped us off at our apartment.

The first bedroom was in the front, with a long hallway leading to a second bedroom, the living room, and a small kitchen. The windows and doors had wooden slats that opened to a view of the street below. Looking down from the balcony, I observed many men sitting at a small bar across the street. I realized that the piazza wasn't the only place men congregated. They seemed to hang out in cliques, each in their own little group, playing cards or just talking.

We put on our walking shoes and followed the Good Friday procession to a small courtyard where we viewed a statue of Jesus on a cross, set on a stone platform. A string of lights ran along the edges for nighttime viewing. Below his feet were roses, baby's breath, and large vases adorning both sides of the platform. There was an open altar with a basket for donations. The people made their way up to the front to throw in their euros and get a better view.

Searching for a restaurant recommended by some Sciacca cousins, we headed to the port. Along the way, we met a man who told us the tale of the Madonna found at sea, but it was a different story from what Cousin Rita had told me. He did say she was brought up in one of the fishing nets, but claimed that the fishermen displayed her in the piazza. Many people were getting sick and dying from the plague at the time. When the townspeople came to see the statue, smoke began to pour from the base of the statue, and the epidemic came to an end. The story has many variations, but this one is the most interesting.

We had lunch at the *Trattoria Al Faro*. In the lobby, there was a tank filled with live fish. You chose your meal before you sat at the table. Since everything was cooked to order, it took longer to get our food than at other restaurants, but it was worth it. Knowing the fish had been alive less than an hour before made it taste even better.

After climbing stairs and hills, Maria was exhausted, so she returned to the room to rest. Marianna and I walked to the Comune to find information about our great-grandparents. The city couldn't find anything on our great-grandmother. They told us to come back after the Easter holiday.

Revived after her nap, Marie was ready to walk again. I led them to the area where our family had lived. As we neared the top of the road, I noticed our Cousin Maria's curtain was open, which meant she was home. She was surprised to see me again and delighted to meet Marianna, who spoke fluent Italian. They talked while Marie and I sat by, trying to understand random Italian words that flew over our heads. Marie had an advantage, though, because she knew Spanish.

Maria showed us a picture of a family gathering. On the wall, in the background, hung a portrait of our great-grandfather, Paolo, but Cousin Maria didn't know who had taken it.

Cimiteriale Comunale - Sciacca

Crypts and Stones

The next day, one of the men downstairs at the bar was singing and shouting in the street. He may not have been right in the head because the other men were very tolerant of his rantings, but I soon learned to recognize his voice at seven o'clock each morning. He became my alarm clock and the signal that the bar was now open for me to buy a cappuccino.

Another cousin, Santo, picked us up from the apartment and drove us to the cemetery. His father was Calogero, one of Maria's nine children. Armed with information about Paolo, Marianna asked the man in the office to help her find his gravesite. They scoured handwritten records bound in tattered covers that probably hadn't seen the light of day in years. I couldn't understand the conversation, but when Marianna jumped up and down with delight, I knew she had found our great-grandfather. She snapped a picture of the record, and I did the same with my camera.

The record gave us a general idea of where Paolo Corrao might be buried, but we didn't find the grave.

The groundskeeper suggested his body may have been exhumed, claiming that cemetery space was at a premium. Unless the family was affluent enough to buy a mausoleum or plot, which could cost as much as a house, grave space was available on a rental basis. If the family didn't renew the lease every ten years, the cemetery had the right to dig up their relatives and use the grave for someone else. The remains are placed in an ossuary, a small container the size of a shoebox, or doused with disintegrating chemicals and buried in a mass grave. I was surprised that there were no apparent records of this. Everything was recorded in a blue cloth-covered book, but it was handwritten and unreadable.

Santo gave us a tour of his aunts and uncles' graves, all children of Nonna Maria Ruffo. Afterward, he invited us to his house for lunch. Santo's house was at the highest level of the tiered community I visited with Rita. She had shown me the home I thought my grandfather grew up in, but it was his sister Maria's house. She lived with her husband, Salvatore Ruffo, and they brought up nine children in such a small house. Against the neighbors' warnings, Marianna squeezed through the narrow gap in the door and entered to take a picture of the upper room.

Santo's wife, Giusy, pronounced Jew-zy, prepared us a delicious pasta lunch with zucchini pesto sauce. On the table was fennel, or as they call it, finocchio, which seemed to be a staple at every meal. They served thick slices of crusty bread drenched in olive oil pressed from the fruit of their olive trees and sprinkled with fresh oregano from their garden. They seemed to use it more than parsley. While we ate, their son, Calogero, watched The Simpsons on television. It was funny to hear Homer and Bart speaking Italian.

For dessert, they put out fresh oranges and pears. I remembered the same custom from my childhood. My mother always put out a tray of fruit and nuts at the end of the meal. My grandfather sat at the table, peeling an orange and cracking walnuts with his arthritic fingers.

Once the meal was over, Calogero gave us a tour of his ceramic workshop, then took us to a house with a shiny wooden door. It was the house where our grandfather and his sisters lived as children. The residents invited us inside. The house had been renovated with modern furniture. We were surprised to find a storage room left intact from the 1890s.

We sat around the large dining room table to drink espresso. I imagined my great-grandfather seated at the head, with my grandfather and his two sisters and my grandmother serving food from the small kitchen. A china cabinet was similar to my mother's, but the teacups were displayed on their side. My mother always set them upright, but doing it the Sicilian way made more sense because dust couldn't collect in them. We ate sweets complemented by fresh ricotta on the side, which had always graced my mother's Sunday dinner table to accompany the pasta. I never ate it outside of that, but I'm learning many uses for that cheese. Marianna even spreads it on her sandwiches.

Everyone has a unique way of pronouncing ricotta. In New York, my family and the Italian community used to say, Re-goth! When I moved to Georgia, I felt silly calling it by its slang. I learned to call it ricotta, like *cot*. Marianna corrected me and insisted I pronounce ricotta with a long o sound. Every time I used the word, I ended up with all three versions — one that the South drummed into my head, one for New York, and one for Sicily.

View from our Apartment

Buona Pasqua

When I woke up in Sciacca on Easter morning, I watched one of the processions heading down the street from my balcony. We were invited to Santo's sister's house for dinner, another woman named Maria. First, we planned to walk to the piazza to see the Easter celebrations. A group of men carried a platform with a statue of Jesus to parade around the town. The two statues were reunited when they arrived at the piazza, where another group waited with Mary. I felt the energy in the air. Even the man who sang at the bar seemed more exuberant.

The crowds had already formed by the time we arrived. Explosions of fireworks mixed with the smell of gunpowder and sea air, and cheers rang out as colorful confetti rained down from a blue sky. In the distance, we could see the two statues raised high in joyous celebration.

We arrived at Cousin Santo's sister's house, and were greeted by their ninety-eight-year-old mother, Giuseppina. She was the wife of the late Calogero and the last surviving relative from that generation.

As we sat around the table, Marianna spoke fluent Italian. We didn't understand most of the conversation, but learned that Sciacca women wore black when their husbands were at sea on fishing boats. Sometimes they were gone for months.

Easter dinner started with pasta in cream sauce, followed by Braciole, a beef roll layered with prosciutto, filled with breadcrumbs and seasonings, and slow-cooked in tomato sauce. There was also a variety of cheeses, sliced meats, and a large bowl of olives. For dessert, we drank espresso, and our hosts brought out the largest dish of cannoli I'd ever seen. My American cousin Marie looked like she was in heaven. We had to snap a picture of her eyeing the tray before her. The meal was finished with a large steaming pot of tea with fennel, lemon slices, and a bay leaf. They said it was a digestive tea.

It was midnight when we returned to our apartment. I was getting ready to jump into bed when I heard music, so I went out onto my balcony and looked down the street. A traffic jam of cars had backed up to our building. People were everywhere! Curious, I quickly got dressed again and went to check it out. I followed the sounds of a live band and arrived at a local outdoor restaurant.

After a quiet day of religious introspection, Sciacca seemed to come alive. Young people were singing and dancing. I stood at the back of the crowd. It was incredible to be part of this musical event. I was exhausted and knew I couldn't stay much longer.

As I turned to leave, I noticed a familiar couple to my left. It was Giovanni and his wife, Natasha. I smiled at her, and she recognized me immediately. We embraced, and I tried to say a few words in Italian. Natasha knew a little English, but it wasn't enough to hold a conversation, so I excused myself and returned to the apartment with another reason to love Sciacca.

Flavors of Sciacca

The day after Easter was a major holiday. Italians called it Pasquetta, or Little Easter. It was also known as *Lunedi dell'Angelo,* Monday of the Angels. All of the stores and most of the restaurants closed for the holiday. It was a day to spend outdoors with family and friends, usually with a picnic at the beach or in the country. Even a roadside meadow was the perfect place to lay out a blanket and eat leftovers from Easter dinner, especially plenty of hard-boiled eggs in bright spring colors. I realized I hadn't seen one Easter basket or chocolate bunny in Sciacca. Instead, the stores set up large displays of chocolate eggs in all sizes, wrapped in cellophane and tied with bows. The egg is the main symbol of the holiday and is the centerpiece of many Pasquetta dishes. Braided bread loaves were baked with a colorful egg in the center, something I remembered from childhood. I had always wondered how we would eat the bread since the egg still had its shell. Funny how a child's mind works. Along with the leftovers from Easter dinner, Heaping trays of steaks and sausages were grilled.

After the meal and a friendly football game, music filled the air, and preparations began for homemade pizza. I was surprised that most of my Italian relatives had a pizza oven in their kitchens, but none of them seemed to have a microwave oven. I think I like their priorities better.

Finally, Jane and Billy arrived a little travel-worn but excited to be in our grandfather's territory. We stayed up late talking and drinking wine, and then we got up early the following day to go sightseeing. I was thrilled to show them all the places I had found during my previous trips.

Billy wanted to see the beach, so we headed down the stairs to the piazza and walked to the port. It was windy, so we stopped at a seaside bar. Billy had a gelato, but Jane and I, being 'winos,' decided on a glass of merlot. We walked a little further, but deterred by the wind, we turned back to town. We saw older men everywhere, walking with their hands behind their backs.

"They all remind me of Grandpa," I said. "That's the way he used to walk."

Billy laughed. "I think they walk like that because it's easier on the inclines."

"Oh," I said, "That makes sense." I put my hands behind my back as we continued walking. It worked!

Since we were all a little hungry, we headed to a restaurant I had visited, which served good pizza but was closed until dinner. The only place I knew of that was open during siesta was the food trucks near the park. Rita had taken me there for a pani e panelle. The thought of fresh calamari tentacles fried to a golden brown made my mouth water.

We noticed that the Basilica doors were open and stopped to light a candle for our mothers, but they weren't like those we remembered from childhood. They were little lights shaped like candles with a switch on the bottom. The church staff shut them off at the end of the day. I don't know if it was a modern technological update or if real candles were a fire hazard. We switched one on and threw some euros into the collection box.

At the front of the church, a large baptismal font once used for infant baptisms stood on a platform. We imagined our grandfather being immersed in the water, just as our families practiced in Brooklyn.

The sacrament of baptism began with John the Baptist and continued through the messianic movement led by Jesus. In early Christian practice, the head was fully submerged underwater, just as it was in our grandparents' time. Since then, other methods have been used, such as affusion (pouring water over the head) or aspersion (sprinkling it).

Famiglia Per Sempre

We were excited about the party our cousins had planned for us that evening and weren't sure what to expect. Cousin Calogero picked us up, and we drove to the restaurant, the same place that was closed at lunchtime. We'd be having that pizza after all.

There were already about thirty cousins inside, and they just kept coming! There were so many of us that we took over the whole restaurant. No one spoke English. I was in a sea of unfamiliar chatter, but the excitement was overwhelming. Everyone knew about the cousins from America. We felt like celebrities as they snapped pictures with us.

Four long tables set with beautiful dinnerware and yellow napkins stretched out in the center of the restaurant. Large bottles of water, natural with a red cap and *gassata* with a blue cap, were arranged around the flowers in the center of the tables, along with large bowls of lemon slices. Of course, no party is complete without Coke, and bottles of it were plentiful.

I never cared for soda but grew fond of gassatta and preferred it to plain water. The smell of baking pizza filled the air, and soon, waiters came out with wooden boards laden with crust, sauce, cheese, and multiple toppings.

The gathering resembled the many Italian weddings I attended in my youth. Young and old alike sat around the tables, drinking and catching up on events. We learned that these get-togethers weren't unusual for our family, and they made a point to meet at least two times a year. My American cousins and I sat at the head table, and a procession of family members came by to greet us. They gave us bear hugs, and we kissed their cheeks. Calogero presented each of us with a large ceramic dish he had made.

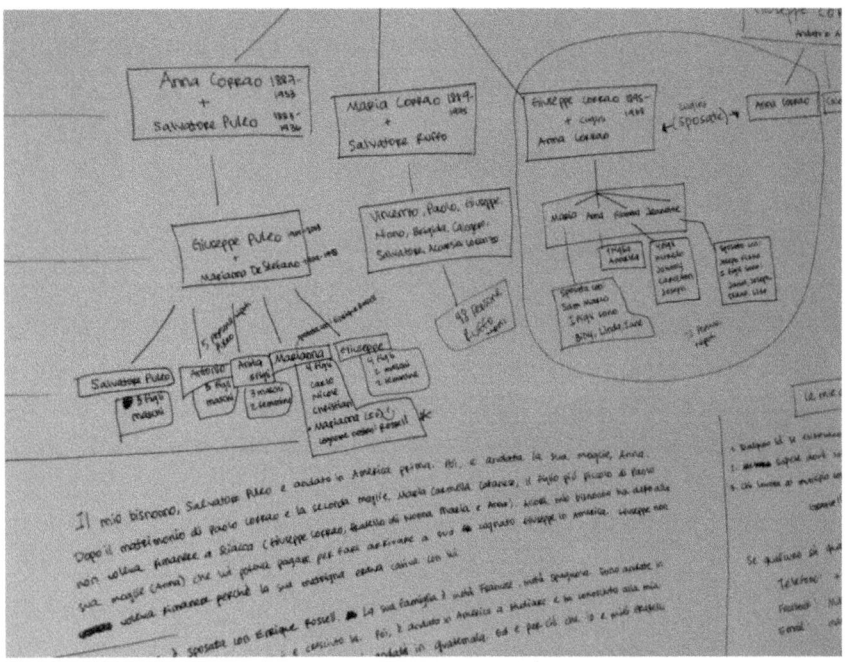

As everyone ate and drank, Cousin Marianna assembled a large bulletin board of our family tree and then displayed it in front of the tables. Everyone crowded around to find their names and confirm our connection.

At the end of the night, the waiters wheeled out two large cakes. The message was in Italian but translated as," Together for a short time, but family forever." We huddled around the cakes and took a group picture. The love surrounding us was incredible. It was a night we would all remember forever.

La Famiglia Maria Corrao Ruffo

The Grotto

The next day, Billy, Jane, and I searched for the Grotto that Rita and I had found last time I was in Sciacca. We arrived and took pictures after weaving through the narrow roads. We stopped off at a drugstore on the way back to our apartment. There was a makeup display, and I picked up an Italian mascara and liner and headed toward the checkout. I misread the cost, and the bill was steep, so I dug through my purse for my credit card. It wasn't there!

Marianna had suggested we keep our passports at the apartment, so I left mine in the front pocket of my suitcase. I thought that maybe my card was with it. I paid for the items with euros and immediately searched for my card when we got home. That's when I began to panic. It was the only card I took on the trip, so I had no money without it! I immediately thought to call the bank and reissue a new card, but we were leaving in the morning. I remembered the last time I used it at the shopping center two days before. I considered running the thirty-minute walk back to the store, but it was only 3:30. I had another hour and a half before the store reopened after siesta.

Billy offered to come with me, but he first wanted an hour's nap. At 4:30, he was sound asleep, and I didn't have the heart to wake him, so I flew out the door and power-walked down the street. Halfway down the block, I ran right into my cousin Accursio. I explained my situation in broken Italian, and he insisted on walking me to the store. I welcomed the company since he could translate for me. We marched to the counter, and he told the clerk about my card. She nodded and opened the register. Feeling hopeful, I waited for my credit card to appear, but it didn't.

We left the store, and Accursio pointed to some apartments. *"Mia figlia vive lì…* my daughter lives there."

Accursio's daughter understood a little English, but he explained in Italian. We piled into her car and drove into town. The only other place I might have left the card was the supermercato down the street from my apartment, so Accursio ran inside to ask.

"*Spero che sia lì* … I hope it's there," I said, but the look on Accursio's face told me I needed to call the credit card company and stop the card.

I kissed his daughter goodbye and said, "Grazie," then Accursio and I walked back to my apartment. As we sat in the kitchen talking to my other cousins, I decided to check my bags one more time and excused myself to go to the room. I emptied my purse on the bed, but the card wasn't there. As I tucked everything back inside, I felt something. It was my credit card, which had slipped through a rip in the lining. Ecstatic, I ran into the kitchen to share the good news. That was a narrow escape. Billy suggested I take a picture of the card's front and back, so I pulled out my phone to take a picture.

San Biagio

There is a town one hour from Sciacca called San Biagio Platani. They have a tradition called the Arches of Bread. During the 18th century, town rulers used a portion of the harvest to decorate the city. Every Easter, residents build towering structures made entirely of bread, rice, beans, pasta, dried fruits, spices, and grains. Each ingredient has a symbolic meaning. The bread represents the body of Christ. Mosaic motifs such as stars, the moon, and the sun are displayed along with white doves symbolizing Christianity. At first, the bread was distributed among the poor, but the tradition later shifted to preservation. The dough is coated with a natural resin, making the food inedible but weatherproof.

San Biagio

On Good Friday, they symbolize grief with rosemary and replace it with round loaves of bread the night before Easter.

Once again, we sat at the family table for a delicious Sicilian dinner. Santo's wife, Giusy, made coiled sausages with lemon and fresh oregano. They tasted like my mother's recipe and brought me back to childhood. Few people outside New York cooked sausage like that, and I wondered if the recipe had been handed down from Sicily. A large bowl of olives on the table reminded Jane of our grandfather cracking green olives to remove the pits. He would put them in a jar with water and salt to make a brine and soak them for a few days to remove the bitterness. They were always available as a snack.

The evening ran long as we ate and drank. Calogero presented us with yet another gift, a ceramic butterfly. It was small and blue, and the details were exquisite. Underneath, there was a small magnet and his signature, Ruffo.

My daughter sent a message that she was no longer at my apartment. She left the keys with my neighbor, who agreed to take over the care of my cat. Laurel texted that she tried to spend the night in the guest room so Riley wouldn't be alone. After a few hours, she gave up and returned to her apartment. It was just as I feared. Although I loved Riley dearly, he was a pest. For one thing, he would try to bite my cheek while I was asleep, but the worst was the attack on my hand. He wanted to be petted, then suddenly turned on me.

Sunrise in the Piazza

My Heart is in Sciacca

We were heading north to Taormina in the morning. I had always wanted to visit there, but I didn't come to Sicily to sightsee. I was writing a book about Sciacca, not Taormina. Besides, we had just met cousins we didn't know existed a year ago. After over a year of researching my ancestry, I wanted to know them. Even with the language barrier, the connection was clear. It was too soon. I didn't want to leave.

I couldn't shut my brain off and lay awake most of the night. At five-thirty, I gave up and dressed to walk and watch the sunrise. Standing in the piazza, I knew what I had to do. I had to break away from the comfort of traveling with my cousins and remain in Sciacca. This wasn't part of my plan, but there was so much more to see.

As soon as I made up my mind, I felt lighter than a feather. All I had to do was break the news to Marie, Marianna, Billy, and Jane.

As I walked back to the apartment, the fragrance of gardenias enveloped my senses. I looked up at the source, a tree covered with white blossoms. I'd never seen gardenia trees, but this was Sicily. There were many different plant species.

At a second glance, I spotted an orange. Imagine that! Orange trees grew along the streets—free for anyone to pick. I reached up and picked one. Peeling off the skin, I took a bite and wrinkled my nose. Their bitter taste wasn't as appealing as their scent. Maybe they weren't ripe yet. They were orange blossoms, delicate and fragrant. I broke off a branch with a cluster of tiny flowers to inhale their sweet scent. I saved them for Marianna, hoping they'd soften the blow when I told her I wasn't joining them.

Jane and Billy were the first I told. Both were loving and sweet and didn't make me feel guilty.

"Do what makes you happy," Billy said.

Then I broke the news to Marie. She informed Marianna, which was a bit of a relief.

Breakfast was unusual—spaghetti and pistachio pesto. I had planned to take the pesto home with me, but I knew the TSA would confiscate it after checking the weight, just like the pistachio butter I had tried to bring home on my first trip from Sicily. It broke my heart to hand over the unopened jar of green gold, and I couldn't bear losing another nut-based delicacy to the airlines, so I cooked up some pasta and smothered it with pesto. It sure beats eating cheese, although Sciacca had some of the best cheeses I'd ever eaten. My favorite was the fresh ricotta that they sold at the outdoor market.

After breakfast, I helped my cousins pack the rental car and wheeled my suitcase across the street to my new hotel, The Conte Luna. They worried about me being alone.

"I'll be fine." I gave them a reassuring smile. "I'll meet up with you next week in Palermo. I'd still have a few days before our flight home."

The Crypt Keeper

At the Conte Luna B&B, I set up my computer to write, happy I finally had decent Wi-Fi. I felt a little isolated, so I took a break to buy groceries at the supermercato. As I walked through the piazza, I spotted Jane.

"What are you doing here?" I asked. "I thought you left."

"Marianna wanted to get some information at the Comune," she said. "Billy and Marie are waiting in the car, but I needed to stretch my legs."

I looked at the city hall building just in time to see her coming out. Beaming, she approached the car. "I have great news," she said. "I was able to get the date of our great-grandmother Maria Colletti's death."

I wrote down the information and promised to find her at the cemetery the next day. Their car drove off, and I felt a twinge of sadness. I'd miss them, but my heart was in Sciacca.

The following day, I woke up with a smile and new energy. When I walked into the dining area, the other patrons were already feasting on croissants and active in their conversations. The receptionist acted as a waitress and stood behind the coffee bar. I ordered my *cappuccino* and took a pistachio pastry off the buffet table. By the time I sat down, everyone had left except the receptionist. I felt her eyes on me. Without my cousin to translate English into Italian, I was alone. Everything seemed to echo in the silence.

After two cappuccinos, I opened the Google Translator application on my phone. I ventured out to find my great-grandmother, Maria Colletti. All I had was her date of death, but Marianna had already sent the information to Francesco. He was the man at the cemetery who helped us find the death records for our great-grandfather, Paolo.

Along the way, I looked up to see the name Colletti on a storefront awning. Maybe it was a sign. I convinced myself that today, after countless times at the cemetery, I would find her.

No one was in the office when I arrived, so I walked around the cemetery and waited until someone showed up. Even with my translator, the man in the office didn't understand me. I was getting a little frustrated at the thought of leaving empty-handed again. Then I spotted Francesco coming through the gate. With the help of my phone translator, I explained that I was Marianna's cousin. His eyes lit up with understanding.

Remembering how helpful he was when Marianna hugged him, we greeted him, exchanging hugs.

He told me to come back after two p.m. Discouraged, I walked the thirty minutes back to town, but I was back promptly at one-forty-five.

He wrapped me in another hug. Boy, did he smell!

We went back into the office, and he pulled out a registry of burial dates. As he thumbed through the worn, handwritten pages, I looked at his hands and noticed dirt under his fingernails. I imagined that he had just dug someone's grave. Francesco found the records for Maria Colletti, who passed away in 1904, and let me take a picture of the document.

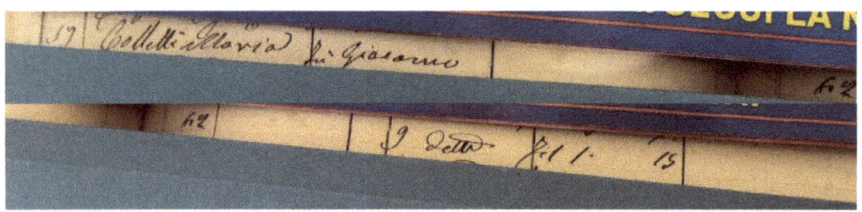

He led me to the same mausoleum that Cousin Rita and I had found in September. As I peeked through the cracked glass door at the tombstones that lined the walls, there was no sign of Paolo Corrao. Francesco saw the look on my face and pulled me away, motioning to the backside of the mausoleum. There was a small wooden door with a white cross on top.

"*I tuoi bisnonni sono qui.* Your great-grandparents are here," the gravedigger said.

Back of the Corrao Family Tomb

I tried looking through the small square windows but couldn't see anything.

"*Perché sono qui?* Why are they here?" I asked.

"*Sono tombè vecchie.* The tomb is old," he said.

I knew that vecchie meant old, but there was no tomb marker.

We went back to the front of the mausoleum. He pointed to a photo of a couple on the left side of the tomb.

"*Quelle sono le tue foto dei bisnonni,*" he said. "Those are your great-grandparents."

Even though I was hopeful, I was also skeptical. There was no nameplate, nothing to mark that my grandparents were there. I was getting suspicious of Francesco's motives, but kept it to myself.

"Who is the man above them?" I asked. "*Chi e l'uomo sopra di loro?*"

"*Quello è Pasquale Corrao.* That is Pasquale Corrao."

"Who is that?" I asked, turning my attention to the photo on the right side of the tomb. "*Chi è quello?*"

"*Quello è il fratello Giovanni.* That is his brother Giovanni."

The placard outside the mausoleum said *Fratelli Corrao* or Corrao brothers, so I didn't question his facts. Now, I knew of four brothers, three in the crypt and their brother Giuseppe, who relocated to America.

Francesco hugged me, and I expected to exit the cemetery, but he had other ideas. He insisted on showing me around the cemetery, and how could I refuse? The sun was warm, and I didn't mind the tour. First, he took me to a tomb with photos of an older man and his very young wife. He rubbed his fingers together, indicating that the man had money.

As we strolled between the graves and crypts, I told him I was a writer. He told me he was a vagabond. Vagabond? Did he live at the cemetery? I was starting to feel uneasy, but the tour wasn't over. He led me to another tomb.

He translated on his cracked phone screen that the man was a writer and was killed by the Mafia. He smiled wide, showing missing and yellow teeth.

"Forse che potrebbe succedere a voi... Maybe that will happen to you," he joked.

Although it was true that my writing had gotten me into trouble on more than one occasion, I didn't think it was funny but tried to laugh it off.

He hugged me as we continued walking among the Italian rich and pointed out the tombs of politicians and crooked businesspeople. These crypts and mausoleums were more elaborate, and he rubbed his fingers together again.

The cemetery was vast, and we were far from the front entrance. The crypt keeper led me to some stairs that went underground, explaining that rising water had damaged the tombs. Francesco then led me to another set of stairs to reach the higher monuments. It was, indeed, a beautiful view. He motioned that I get on the scaffolding for a good photo of the grounds. Feeling brave but stupid, I let Francesco steady me as I climbed up to take a few shots. He was all too eager to help me down, his grip lingering uncomfortably.

It was all fascinating, but I was starting to get nervous. I wondered if the other man was still in the office or if we were all alone. I told him that I needed to leave soon, but Francesco kept stalling. I got my bearings by the windmill in the distance, so I knew I'd find my way out. I somehow guided us to the front of the cemetery by pretending to be interested in specific paths. He led me to another area with beautiful trees and sat on a wall, motioning for me to join him.

Francesco got creepier from there. He kept making jokes and pretending to push me over the edge of a railing. Then he hugged me to him and laughed. What was there to stop him from raping me and throwing me in an open grave?

Nothing!

I wondered if I'd make it out alive or end up finding my great-grandfather, Paolo, after all.

When we got close to the front, I told him I had seen enough dead people for one day and that I had to leave.

"*Devo davvero andarmene,*" I said. "I have to leave."

But he didn't seem to care. I sensed danger but tried to logic my way out.

I promised I'd come back the next day. That old ploy never fails me when I'm in a jam. I don't think Francesco believed me, but he let me go. His eyes stayed on me as I walked out of the gate. I waved once. Then, the second I turned the corner, I ran for my life.

I wasn't even three blocks away from the cemetery when I saw a woman walking toward me on the side street. She looked familiar. As she came closer, we both stopped. It was Cousin Maria.

"I thought you left," she said in Italian and looked like she saw a ghost.

I explained I had decided to stay behind in Sciacca. Soon, all my cousins found out.

Olive Farm in the Country

Cugini

Word spread that I had remained in Sciacca. Everywhere I went, I heard horns beeping at me. At first, I thought I had violated some traffic rules, but I quickly realized that these cousins recognized me from the party. I bought two small plants and left them on Maria and Giusy's front steps since they weren't home.

I received a message to come for lunch the next day from Santo and Giusy. I had to make another trip to the bakery for pastries. The owner was getting to know me since I often frequented her shop. With my cellphone fully charged, I climbed the steep incline to the top where their house was. Every time I go there, I have to pass Maria's house. I felt terrible because I wanted to see her too.

The scent of frying fish filled my senses when I entered the door. Giusy was cooking small sardines stuffed with a breadcrumb mixture. The fish, still intact with its head and skin, seemed to stare at me accusingly. I rarely think of eating fish that isn't already filleted by the supermarket and neatly displayed on ice chips in the glass cases.

Giusy placed a rather large bowl of pasta in front of me. It was overflowing with tiny shrimp, which they caught locally. The sauce looked green, like pesto. It was delicious, and just when I thought I couldn't eat another thing, she brought out the sardines. I was a little anxious, but I took one. It was surprisingly tasty. I asked why they were so flavorful. They said it was because the seawater around Sciacca was saltier than the Atlantic.

I felt more Italian than ever, connecting with my Sicilian cousins. I wanted to embrace my culture, but it was hard to communicate because they didn't speak English. At first, my translator worked perfectly, and we conversed, but the signal often dropped, and I was on my own. More and more, I began to think about dual citizenship. It was in my blood, just waiting to get out. I promised my cousins I'd come to Sciacca again in September.

After lunch, Maria came to visit. She insisted it was her turn to have me over and invited me for lunch the next day.

The next day, carrying a small pastry box, I visited Cousin Maria. Her brother, Accursio, came just in time for an espresso.

Afterward, he drove the three of us to see Maria's daughter, Roberta. I was almost speechless when we pulled in front of a sizeable wrought-iron gate. Accursio exited the car to buzz us in, and the gates swung open.

A large modern house loomed in front of us, surrounded by groves of olive trees. Roberta and her husband had an olive business. We drank coffee and ate some homemade treats while their daughter did her homework at the table. I imagined what it was like to be a high school student in Sicily. Did they learn about American history? Politics?

Then, Roberta gave me a tour of the grounds. The olives were green when harvested in September. They turned brown in November and black by December.

She showed me the spacious party room off the patio where they hosted family gatherings. It even had a pizza oven. Wanting any excuse to return, I offered to help with the olive harvest.

After dropping Cousin Maria off at her house, Accursio drove us to the marina. We walked out along the long concrete dock, where people stood fishing in the late afternoon light.

On the Docks of the Marina

It didn't matter what size their catch was. All the fish went into the fishermen's buckets. There didn't seem to be rules like back in the States, where certain fish had to be specific sizes, and anyone trying to sneak away with protected marine life could be slapped with a hefty fine. I don't even think a fishing license was required. At first, no requirements seemed good, but then I noticed all the trash lined up along the dock. Sciacca has a daily cleaning crew for the streets. I saw them every morning, rolling back and forth with the large circular brushes on the bottom of their trucks, scooping up garbage and sweeping the road. The docks were a different story. The cleaning crew couldn't keep up with the trash the sailors threw overboard since their trucks only went out once a week. Piled along the side, it attracted birds and rodents. I guess we all have to eat.

After pondering this and other aspects of Sicilian anglers, we drank coffee at a small café near Porta Salvatore. I was familiar with Porta Palermo because it had wooden doors, which were once used to control traffic. I knew about others, Porta San Pietro, Porta Calogero, Porta del Mare, and Porta dei Bagni, but I hadn't noticed their locations.

We drank espresso and watched the children playing in the same schoolyard that Accursio played in as a child. It was an old school, probably the very one that my grandfather and his sisters attended. It was getting late, and Accursio had the night shift at the train station as a conductor.

On the way home, we passed by a stone wall. I asked Accursio what it was, and he was surprised that I didn't know about Luna Castle. He pulled up to the front entrance, but the sign on the castle said closed. We noted the hours of operation, and Accursio said, "Domani."

Outer walls of the Castle

Castello Luna

Accursio came to pick me up to go to the castle, but I wanted to go to the outdoor market since it was Saturday morning. I had passed it the prior week during a trip to the cemetery, but we didn't stop. I knew the general area but wasn't sure how to get there.

    I was lost and walked through the winding streets, asking random people for directions, then followed the smell of chickens roasting. The scent mingled with fresh bread and pastries. This market was an array of tastes: olives, cheese, nuts, and vegetables. After taking it all in, I mapped my route back to town.

Only two blocks from Conte Luna B&B was the famous Luna Castle. Built on solid rock, it stands at the top of the east part of the city, not far from the house where my grandfather grew up. The castle had four parts: the central palace, the defense walls, and two towers. It remained intact until an earthquake damaged it in 1740. Only the base remains today, but the majestic splendor is still evident with its panoramic views of the city. Guglielmo Peralta, a member of the Spanish Luna family, built the castle in 1380. His granddaughter, Margherita, was to marry Giovanni Perollo but was jilted and left at the altar. Her humiliation sparked resentment between the two most powerful families and fueled a bloody feud that lasted two centuries. The castle is open for tours in the spring and sometimes has live music with food and drink set up in the center court.

Not far from the Luna Castle is an enchanted garden called Incantato, built by an eccentric man, Filippo Bentivegna. He grew up in a poor family in Sciacca. He ran away to America at twenty to avoid military service under Mussolini. After facing racism in America and a beating by a rival suitor, he returned to Sciacca. The police caught up with him, and he was arrested. The authorities decided he wasn't mentally fit to stand trial and released him. Filippo never married. Using the money he earned in America, he purchased land outside of the town, where he lived a solitary life, painting and chiseling images of heads in stone and on the trees in his sculpture garden.

He also built caves and alcoves, decorating their exteriors with sculpted heads, and proclaimed himself the "Lord of the Caves." Upon his death, the garden was opened to the public. After nearly a thousand of the sculpted heads were stolen, security was tightened to better protect the site and regulate tourism.

"Io scavo queste caverne e penetro nella terra…io la possiedo ne traggo forza ed energia e per questo qui sono tutti vivi…"
Filippo Bentivegna

"I dig these caverns and penetrate the earth … I own it, and I draw strength and energy, and for this reason, everyone here is alive …" Filippo Bentivegna.

Recca

Marianna sent me a message: a family member who helped maintain the Corrao mausoleum had agreed to meet us, and she decided to return to Sciacca for one day. I met her at the bus stop, and together we waited for the man who might finally give us answers. His name was Giacomo. He and Marianna chatted in Italian while I sat quietly in the back seat, wishing I understood what was being said. I hoped she'd fill me in later.

We drove to the cemetery. I felt a flicker of unease at the thought of seeing the crypt keeper again, though I suspected he'd now fixate on my beautiful young cousin. As we walked the dirt path, his tone had changed. He admitted he wasn't sure whether our grandparents were truly buried in the mausoleum. Giacomo opened the door, and we stepped inside to take photos.

Afterward, we got back into his car and drove to visit his father, Agostino Recca, who owned an international company that exports Sciacca fish and other local products. After a brief tour of the facility, we were invited into a small office to meet Agostino himself. He was older but still sharp, clearly running the business with confidence. Marianna continued the conversation in Italian while I sat quietly again, frustrated by the language barrier. I promised myself I would learn Italian.

We posed for a group photo before driving off. Though I still couldn't confirm the exact family connection, I surmised it must be through marriage, since the tomb held our great-great-great-grandfather Pasquale and his brother Giovanni, whose faces appeared in the photographs. On the way back to town, I stared out the window, lost in thought — until I spotted the familiar vendor where I always bought calamari from the *Pani e Panelle* truck. He looked up and caught my eye with a puzzled expression, as if trying to place where he'd seen me before.

My trip had come to an end, and I said *arrivederci* to Sciacca, knowing I would return in the fall. But first, I had to have one more calamari for the road. Wouldn't you know it? My friend on the motor scooter was right there, watching me eat. His name was Giuseppe. When I finished, he pulled out a package of tissues and offered me one.

"Who is that?" Marianna asked.

"Oh, some guy who always seems to show up when I'm near the park. I don't think he works—he's always here."

Marianna and I loaded our suitcases and climbed onto the bus to Palermo, where Jane and Marie were waiting before our flight back to the States.

Just before the bus departed, Giuseppe boarded and made his way to the back to hand me more tissues and sneak in another hug. I was speechless, but Marianna was not.

"*Vai fuori di qui!*" she shouted.

Stunned, Giuseppe obeyed and got off the bus. I thought that would be the last of him, but I was wrong. I'd have to deal with Giuseppe again. Italians are persistent.

Cefalù

The next day, we jumped on a train to the second-largest resort area in Sicily, **Cefalù**, a province of Palermo. The Romans had taken over a small Greek settlement there and used it as a pivotal port to control the Tyrrhenian Sea. The train ride took only an hour. The town was buzzing with people—buses lined the streets, and we wondered what was going on.

We walked through town toward *La Rocca*, a towering crag along the shoreline. Lunch at *La Vecchia Marina* was a bit pricey, but the ambiance made it worthwhile. We had a table overlooking the sea with a perfect view of the crag.

Marianna managed to get us a ride back to town, where large crowds had formed around the church. We stopped to see what all the hoopla was about. It turned out the church was an important seat of one of Sicily's most prominent bishoprics. The head bishop was scheduled to appear and speak to the faithful.

We nestled between the people sitting along the curb and waited for the festivities to begin.

After about half an hour, we caught the next train back to Palermo, eager to return to our apartment. On the way, we picked up a bottle of wine.

As we sat around the kitchen table, the conversation turned to my sister. She was about to be displaced now that our mother was gone. I had been in denial, unable—or unwilling—to accept the reality of her death. Between staying busy with work and planning my trip to Sciacca, I had shoved the truth into a corner of my mind. But now, it hit me full force. My mother was gone.

Everyone seemed to have an opinion about what my sister should do next, but I knew better. Finding a job after more than ten years out of the workforce isn't easy. Things have changed. You can't just walk into a place and fill out an application. Everything is online now, and most of the time, it feels like you're sending your résumé into a black hole. My sister cried as she described the silence, the rejection without even a reply. And the bank wouldn't let her take over the mortgage without proof of income. No job, no house.

Tears welled in my eyes. No one seemed to have any sympathy for her. But I heard my mother's voice in my head as clearly as if she were sitting beside me: *"Take care of Lisa."* And I broke down.

For years, my sister hadn't held a steady job. Instead, she stayed home to care for our mother, who, in turn, had taken out a reverse mortgage just to make ends meet. Now that she was gone, the bank swooped in like a vulture. And the thought of letting my mother down was almost more than I could bear.

Sobbing uncontrollably, I ended the conversation. The others drifted into the living room to watch television. I stayed behind. I just wanted to go to sleep.

Saturday Market

Our last day in Sicily was Saturday, and the outdoor market was teeming with food and last-minute gifts. I picked up some small jars of pistachio cream—this time, TSA wouldn't be able to confiscate them.

We weren't sure what we'd eat, but the food vendors offered plenty of choices. Some had grills sizzling with thick slabs of swordfish and other fish, their heads still intact. Skate sizzled on the grates, wings spread open like fans. They didn't look particularly appetizing, but one delicacy caught my eye: a whole stuffed squid. I made a mental note to try recreating it when I got home.

Behind all the cooking stations were rows of fresh fish laid out for sale. Some were curled head to tail and tied with string, as if caught mid-struggle. Their glassy eyes stared blankly at the passing shoppers.

Hairy Situation

Our last day in Sicily was Saturday, and the outdoor market was teeming with food and last-minute gifts. I picked up a few small jars of pistachio cream—this time, TSA wouldn't confiscate them. While we weren't sure what we'd eat for lunch, the food vendors were out in full force. Grills were set up with thick slabs of swordfish and other fish roasting whole, heads still attached. Skate fish sizzled with their wings stretched wide—less than appetizing—but one delicacy caught my eye: a whole stuffed squid. I made a mental note to try recreating it once I got home. Behind the cooking stalls, rows of fresh fish lay on display. Some were tied head to tail, coiled into strange shapes, their eyes glassy and vacant, as if caught mid-struggle.

On our flight back, we had a stopover in Rome. Marianna was still feeling the effects of the cold she'd had since our arrival. The altitude pressure caused unbearable pain in her ear. By the time we landed, she and her mother decided to stay behind in Rome to see a doctor.

Jane and I flew back to the States together, grateful to be going home, yet already missing each other. After two weeks side by side, it would feel strange not to see her every day. Before we parted, she reminded me to make that dermatologist appointment about my hair.

Once home and settled, I followed through. The dermatologist gave me a long list of supplements—Viviscal (made from shark cartilage), flaxseed capsules, vitamin D, biotin, and Rogaine. She also prescribed Spironolactone, a diuretic meant to block the male hormone that causes hair loss.

I normally avoided medication, but this felt different. Desperate for answers and encouraged by the plan, I dropped off the prescription.

It was shaping up to be a full summer. Though I was still mourning my mother, I had plenty to focus on. My business was thriving, and I was excited about my volunteer work. First came the Vero Beach Air Show. I had signed up months in advance when I heard they needed volunteers. The Blue Angels were scheduled to return after a tragic cancellation the year before — one pilot had died in an accident. This year, they were in rare form, and I had front-row seats.

Soon after came the Vero Beach Wine and Film Festival. It was my third year, and I served as venue captain for the Theatre Guild. But just a week before the event, I began noticing more hair in the shower. At first, I ignored it, but when it kept happening, I started photographing the clumps collecting in the sink. Something felt wrong.

It was time to start the higher dose of Spironolactone, but something stopped me. I went online to look up side effects, just in case. That's when I found a blog full of horror stories from women who swore the drug made their hair fall out. My heart dropped. I stopped taking it immediately and called the doctor to make another appointment.

When I confronted her, she dismissed my concerns. "It's not from the medication," she insisted. "You have alopecia." She suggested a biopsy to confirm. I was still in shock — why hadn't she done that before prescribing the drug? But I agreed. She numbed the top of my scalp and took a sample.

"Will I lose hair in that area?" I asked. It felt like a silly question, considering how much I was already losing.

"Yes," she said without hesitation.

I wish I had asked her to take the sample from the right side, where I already had a cowlick. She warned me the hair in that spot might never grow back.

Dreading the possibility of needing a wig, I began searching for a salon that specialized in hair extensions.

Sicily has three points symbolized by a Trinacrium. The symbol can be seen everywhere around Sicily, with the head of Medusa surrounded by three bent legs and three stalks of wheat.

Sicilian Artisans

My mind kept going back to Sicily. Although I loved my life in Florida, a part of me was tempted to leave everything behind and relocate to my ancestral home. Returning to my Sicilian roots felt like a comforting escape from the chaos of my life. Maybe it was my mother's death, or the deep connection I felt with my newfound family. Before making such a significant decision, I had to be sure it was the right one.

Five months later, I boarded a plane back to Sciacca for the fourth time. I was becoming a pro at it. After a long but pleasant stopover in Zurich, I arrived in Palermo late that evening. I wasn't staying in the city — I had booked a B&B just outside of town.

Tra le Braccia di Morpheo was a small town in the province of Palermo, known for its colorfully painted horse-drawn carts, an art dating back to the seventeenth century. Originally used as a means of transport, the carts are now reserved for special events and festivals. The tradition serves as a nostalgic reminder of days gone by and a symbol of Sicilian folklore. It's a craft that has been closely guarded and passed down from father to son for generations.

The custom of painting carts served various functions. Aside from protecting the wood and prolonging the cart's lifespan, the tradition also had a superstitious element. Some featured religious scenes are believed to have the power to ward off harm. The paintings also served as advertisements for commercial carts—an explosion of color designed to attract potential customers—and as a status symbol, showcasing the owner's wealth. Depending on the region, some carts were rectangular and painted primarily in red, adorned with elaborate floral décor. Even the horses are decorated with wreaths of flowers and ribbons on special occasions.

Although my B&B was only twenty minutes from the airport, it wasn't close to the bus stop. I had to take a taxi and figure out how to reach the central Palermo station, where I would catch the early bus to Sciacca the following morning. The owner told me a local bus left early and offered to take me to the stop after breakfast.

As promised, he dropped me off at the correct location. At first, there weren't many people waiting, but the crowd grew as the bus remained delayed. By the time it arrived, more than twenty people were pushing to get on. I ended up second to last. The driver held out his arm, blocking me.

"L'autobus è pieno," he said.

My heart raced. I might miss the connection to Sciacca.

"Per favore," I pleaded. "Ho bisogno di andare a Sciacca."

A kind young woman intervened, explained my situation, and suggested I stand. Annoyed but willing, the driver flipped down a small seat near him and allowed me to stay, though I had to store my suitcase below. I remembered the last time a bus rode off with my bags, but I had no choice. Thankfully, I got on while others were turned away.

Once I reached Sciacca, I headed straight to my favorite truck stop for calamari. No sign of Giuseppe—until I took a detour through the park. There he was, like clockwork. My heart sank. He hugged me and motioned toward a bench. I told him I was waiting for my cousin, but he lit a cigarette and sat down anyway.

"Mangiare," he said, handing me a napkin.

I did just that, but it was hard to enjoy the food while trying to answer his questions through my translator. Just as I began to feel stuck, Accursio pulled up, saving me once again.

If I had known how beautiful the apartment was, I would've booked it for the whole month. A small balcony overlooked the piazza, and from my bedroom, I could watch the boats coming and going at the marina. When I told the host I planned to stay one extra night to catch the early morning bus to the airport, he agreed and didn't charge me. "It's fine," he said. "I know Accursio."

My cousin should be the mayor. Everywhere we went, people knew him.

Sea Glass

The fishing boats returned to the harbor at dusk, trailed by flocks of seabirds—a sure sign of a plentiful catch.

At five o'clock, Accursio arrived to take me to dinner. We opened a bottle of wine he had brought and spread out the family photographs across the table. As he helped me identify each face, we lost track of time. His wife, Giovanna, was waiting, so we packed up the pictures and headed out.

Dinner was a feast. We began with tender beef and potatoes, then moved on to delicate fish rolls filled with seasoned breadcrumbs, savory platters of olives, and a fragrant couscous. For dessert, we shared a gelato roll—half chocolate, half pistachio. I skipped the bread, wanting to save room for the good stuff.

After dinner, we sipped coffee on their balcony beneath the full moon. From there, they pointed to San Calogero in the distance. The view was breathtaking, the air soft and still.

Giovanna brought out her coral jewelry collection and opened a picture book of their children's weddings. I hadn't realized that coral was native to Sicily, but the Mediterranean waters are rich in *Corallium rubrum*, one of the world's most prized corals. I've always loved the orange family of hues, and these gems—formed over decades by tiny, tentacled polyps—felt like living fire encased in stone.

Starting white, the coral slowly deepens into brilliant reds in the presence of manganese salts. They grow slowly, spreading just three to four centimeters in ten years under the right conditions—cool, calm waters with little light.

Legends swirl around coral. Some say it was born from the blood of Medusa, daughter of Phorcys. After Perseus severed her head, he laid it on the sea plants. Her blood transformed them, and when they hardened in the air, they became coral. Later, Christian lore reimagined the myth, associating the red coral with Christ's blood and turning it into a sacred symbol. Early paintings show coral worn by infants—even by the baby Jesus—believed to protect them from evil.

For a moment, the past and present blurred. Surrounded by warmth, history, and stories older than I could grasp, I felt deeply at home.

At first glance, Sciacca appears to be an environmentally pristine place. The food packaging is minimal and elegant, and nearly every business displays clearly labeled bins for plastic recycling. But during one of my early morning strolls along the beach, the illusion began to crumble.

The shoreline was scattered with empty bottles, broken glass, and discarded trash—evidence of late-night parties and careless boaters. I felt a tug of responsibility and promised myself I'd return the next day with a garbage bag to do my part. But as I stood there surveying the expanse of litter, it became painfully clear: one person with a trash bag wouldn't be enough. It would take an army to make even a dent. And even then, without a broader cultural shift, the trash would keep coming—beer bottles hurled against the rocks, wrappers floating in with the tide, detritus tossed casually from passing boats.

Sea glass, though often admired for its frosted beauty, is born of this carelessness. Each shard tells the story of a broken bottle, its sharp edges worn down by years of salt and sand. But beauty shouldn't have to rise from recklessness.

There is hope, though—quietly building. In a small but meaningful movement, the youth of Sciacca are beginning to reclaim their coastline. Inspired by Ecopneus, a nonprofit focused on environmental recovery, three hundred secondary school students recently gathered at the Francesco Auditorium. Their goal: to launch a video campaign and open a dialogue centered on a love for their land. They see themselves not just as residents, but as stewards of Sciacca's future.

With support from the mayor and local educators, Ecopneus has led one of the most ambitious cleanup efforts in the province of Catania, collecting over 17,000 tons of recyclable waste across designated stations—entirely free of charge. Their work is transforming not just the landscape but the mindset, turning what was once a public health hazard into sustainable materials that can be repurposed for the greater good.

Progress is slow, but it has begun. And that, perhaps, is how all change starts—not with grand gestures, but with the quiet conviction of a few who refuse to look away.

Termi di Sciacca

I walked slowly past the condominiums and townhouses lining the Mediterranean shore, their balconies catching the last blush of the afternoon sun. A pang of longing tugged at me. Back home, our houses sat in neat, designated communities—row after row of nearly identical façades. Perfect lawns. Timed sprinklers. Symmetry without soul.

What were they missing?

Humanity.

In those neighborhoods, you rarely saw anyone outside unless they were checking the mailbox or walking the dog. The only signs of life came from the slow rise and fall of garage doors as people backed out for work or slipped inside for the night. Even the expensive homes felt sealed off—pristine, untouched, sterile.

Wouldn't it be something to live here? I thought. Maybe buy a little place near Rita, down by Lido Beach.

I stopped for lemon gelato and let the citrusy sweetness lift my mood. Then I made my way to visit Cousin Maria. As always, she insisted on making me spaghetti. I didn't protest. A few minutes later, Accursio arrived just in time for espresso. We spread out more pieces of the family puzzle, trying to stitch together generations with words that didn't always translate cleanly.

Using my phone to interpret was exhausting. Meanings blurred between screens and syllables. But still, I kept trying.

Later that afternoon, Accursio and I drove up to San Calogero, perched on Mount Kronio. The church had been closed the last time I visited, but today, the doors were open, and I stepped inside.

Behind the sanctuary, a stone passage led to the natural steam caves, their entrances carved into the living rock. These ancient baths were built on the slopes of an inactive volcano and date back to the 7th century B.C. Both the Greeks and Romans once soaked here—seeking healing, rest, and ritual here. The air was thick with the scent of minerals, warm and slightly sulfurous. Inside, the spas emitted water vapor from sulfurous and mildly radioactive springs, with temperatures reaching nearly forty degrees Celsius—around 108 degrees Fahrenheit.

In ancient times, these vapors were believed to cure skin conditions, ease rheumatism, and provide relief for respiratory ailments. Standing there, surrounded by walls that had echoed with centuries of breath and prayer, I could almost feel the pulse of the past rise up with the steam.

Photo from http://www.termesciaccaspa.it

Closer to the sea, a sprawling spa complex once stood — part of Italy's Public Healthcare system. Right next door, a hotel welcomed scholars and tourists alike. Known as *Terme di Sciacca*, or *The Molinelli Pools*, the center attracted visitors from around the world, drawn by the promise of healing waters and therapeutic mud baths. These treatments were believed to reduce stress and slow the progression of chronic illnesses.

Thermal therapy was considered a natural remedy for a range of ailments — from female reproductive disorders and fibromyalgia to arthritis, gout, and articular rheumatism. Skin conditions like psoriasis, eczema, seborrheic dermatitis, acne, and even allergic reactions were treated here. The benefits extended to respiratory and lung diseases, making it a cornerstone of holistic care.

For a time, Sciacca emerged from its quiet coastal isolation, drawing wellness seekers and positioning itself as a hub of therapeutic tourism. To meet growing demand, the municipality promoted the construction of a second spa near the railway, in the Cammordino district.

But the momentum didn't last.

Tourism declined. The original spa couldn't sustain itself, and gradually, all thermal activities — and the hotels that depended on them — were suspended. Eventually, the building was sold, marking the end of an era for Sciacca's once-renowned healing waters.

Calogero invited me to dinner with his family, and I arrived with an extravagant chocolate gelato cake I'd picked up from the bakery in town. As we gathered around the table, platters of food were passed, and I filled my plate with a little bit of everything, including the sardines.

Trying to be brave, I cringed slightly and took a bite — head and all.

Crunch.

To my horror, I realized I'd just chewed into a mouthful of bones. I quickly tried to spit them into my napkin as discreetly as possible, but Santo caught me and burst into laughter.

He leaned toward my phone and typed into the translator: "Pull the head off and open the body to take the middle bones out."

"Oh," I said, cheeks burning with embarrassment. Lesson learned — again.

Italian Wedding

Up early, I decided to make a run to the supermercato. Along the way, I ran into Cousin Santo and his wife, Giusy, on their way to work. They stopped to chat and invited me to dinner again before I left Sciacca. Groceries in hand, I cut through a side street toward the piazza — and spotted yet another cousin! Antonia recognized me immediately and ran over with a smile. We both pulled out our translator apps. She was getting married on Tuesday.

Figures. It had to be the day I was leaving. I missed my chance to attend a genuine Italian wedding.

Growing up, I'd been to plenty of weddings, but there's nothing quite like an Italian one. Everything is steeped in tradition—from rituals that promise good fortune to multi-course feasts that go on for hours. It's said that if a bride wears green the night before her wedding, she's ensured good luck. These days, a green ribbon or emerald brooch will do. The best man toasts "*a per cent'anni!*"—to a hundred years—with prosecco or Italian champagne.

Superstitious grooms sometimes carry a piece of iron in their pockets to ward off evil as they wait at the altar. A ribbon across the church doorway signals that a wedding is in progress, drawing in passersby who crowd the back pews to catch a glimpse of the bride's grand entrance. In the U.S., rice is thrown as the couple exits. In Italy, they're met with claps and shouts of *"Auguri!"* And instead of cans trailing from the back of the car, Italians decorate the front grill with flowers.

The ceremony may be sacred, but once it ends, the real focus turns to the food. Guests are treated to as many as twelve courses, beginning with an elaborate buffet. At the end of the meal, each guest receives *confetti*—sugar-coated almonds wrapped in lace—and the cake, *millefoglie*, layers of flaky pastry with vanilla and chocolate creams, often topped with fresh strawberries.

Italian weddings also have their signature dances. Guests link hands and move in a circle, keeping time with the music. As the tempo quickens, so does the pace—until they're spinning so fast, they change direction just to catch their breath.

Instead of wrapped gifts, the bride carries *la borsa*, a satin purse where guests slip in envelopes of money before greeting the couple at the head table with a kiss.

As I passed the Basilica, another wedding was underway. I popped in just in time to watch a bride make her way down the aisle. Later, I snapped photos of another couple posing in the piazza, glowing in the Mediterranean sun.

Accursio picked me up to have breakfast with him and his brother, Emilio, who was visiting from Canada. On the walk to the *pasticceria*, we ran into yet another cousin—Giuseppe, the husband of a relative, who joined us for a cappuccino. Emilio spoke English and even knew of Vero Beach. I invited him to visit. His flight back to Canada was that afternoon, and after a warm goodbye, Accursio and I drove to the highest point in Sciacca: San Michele.

You couldn't go anywhere in Sciacca without running into family.

Sure enough, we found another cousin sitting in a small park along the way. I stood beside Accursio, nodding and smiling while they chatted in Italian. I couldn't follow the conversation, but I took in the breathtaking view of the town below. At the summit were the ancient remnants of Sciacca's old city walls—weathered stone, silent witnesses to centuries of stories, including mine.

Good Medicine

I hadn't planned on learning about the Italian medical system, but the situation presented itself, and I had no choice. I'm not someone who gets sick often, so I had taken my good health for granted. Right in the middle of my trip, though, I started feeling congested and couldn't stop sneezing.

Oh no, I thought. Why now?

I tried every home remedy I could think of—even apple cider vinegar—but nothing was stopping this bug.

I'd been invited to dinner with my friend Josie, but she had two small children, and I didn't want to risk getting them sick. I called to let her know.

"Don't be silly," she said. "We're just going for pizza with my parents, Giovanni's brother Vito, and Cristina's wife."

Planning to quarantine myself at the far end of the table, I accepted. I guess Sicilians have no fear of contamination. Even when I messaged Accursio to say I wasn't up for sightseeing, he came anyway—and insisted on taking me to the doctor.

I was a little nervous. Seeking medical attention in a foreign country, where I didn't speak the language or understand the system, felt daunting.

But I had Accursio.

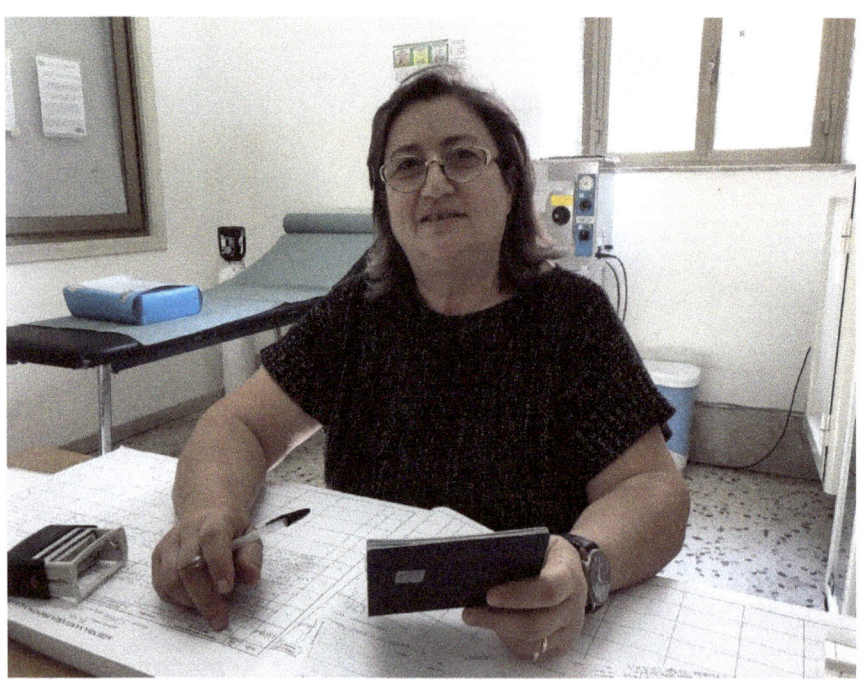

We walked about three blocks to a building I had passed many times without realizing what it was. Accursio rang the bell, and even though it was Sunday, someone answered and led us to the waiting room. It wasn't long before the doctor called us in.

As Accursio translated my symptoms, the doctor took my blood pressure and examined my throat. Within minutes, she handed over a prescription for an antibiotic. The visit cost sixteen euros, payable at the post office the next day.

Sixteen euros. I was stunned.

Sicily offers both public and private healthcare systems. Most emergency hospitals operate under the national public system. And if you need an ambulance, don't dial 911—here, the emergency number is 112.

As we stepped outside, Accursio casually pointed across the street to another building I'd passed countless times. "That's the prison," he said.

Suddenly, the street I thought I knew held a very different meaning.

Accursio dropped me off at my apartment and reminded me to eat something with the antibiotic. After a short rest, I decided to head out and find a toy store to pick up gifts for Josie's daughters. I kept a cautious eye out for Giuseppe. Sure enough, there he was—standing in front of a coffee vendor with an espresso cup in hand.

I quickly crossed the street, praying he wouldn't see me.

I thought I was in the clear—until I heard him shout my name.

Pretending not to hear, I picked up my pace and turned up a steep stone stairway that led to another street. Huffing and puffing by the time I reached the top, I paused to catch my breath. There was the toy store—just ahead.

But so was something else.

A motor scooter was zipping in my direction. Giuseppe. He had outsmarted me by taking another route to the top. Beads of sweat dripped from his forehead as he approached.

"Janet!" he called, as if it were fate that brought us together again. He reached out for a hug.

"No, Giuseppe! Io sono malata!" I said firmly, yanking a tissue from my purse like a sword. He didn't budge. I said it again—this time in English. "I don't feel well!"

That got his attention. He blinked, stunned. "Va bene, Janet."

Before he could say anything else, I waved him off. "A domani," I said, knowing full well I'd be long gone before he realized I wasn't coming back.

At least one good thing had come out of being sick—it gave me the perfect excuse to avoid another awkward encounter. But now I was craving hot soup—something restorative and soothing.

A quick Google search led me to *La Bottega del Porto*, a harbor-side restaurant with a five-star rating. One tourist called their fish stew "the best they'd ever tasted." My mouth watered. *Zuppa di Pesce*—just what I needed.

Then I saw the hours. **CLOSED ON MONDAY.**

Standing at the corner near my apartment, clutching gifts for the girls, I waited for Josie and Giovanni to pick me up for dinner with their family. The pizzeria lot was packed, a nightly ritual in Sciacca. Drivers double-parked their cars to dash inside for takeout. Every few minutes, a horn blared—

Good Medicine | 237

someone blocked in, waiting for the offender to scurry out with a pizza box and move their car.

The place clearly had a loyal following. I'd walked past it a dozen times but never stopped in. Now I made a mental note to try a slice before heading home. In Sciacca, I hadn't met a pizza I didn't like.

Thankfully, I'd stopped sneezing and felt a little better, but I still kept my distance out of caution. Josie and Giovanni took turns tending to their youngest daughter, passing her between bites. Then she was passed along to Vito, Christina, and Josie's mother so Josie could eat in peace.

Carlo, Josie's father, spoke English, which let me relax a bit and enjoy the conversation. Italian words floated around me, and to my surprise, I was starting to understand more. Maybe there was hope for me yet.

Christina's husband, Vito, was already out for a drink at Tinchitè, a small bar near the piazza. Josie convinced her mother to take the girls for a sleepover, giving us an excuse to join them and enjoy a rare adult evening.

Sciacca is a town of fishermen and tourists by day, but at night, it belongs to the young. The streets pulsed with energy. It felt like a festival, even though it was just a regular night. We grabbed a table outside, and Giovanni ordered wine.

As the evening wore on, the weariness crept in again. My body hadn't caught up with my spirit. Just as I debated how to excuse myself without sounding like a downer, Josie got a call—little Gloria wouldn't stop crying. She wanted her mamma.

Relieved by the perfect out, I hugged Josie goodnight and walked home. But even hours later, the town kept partying. At two a.m., I peeked out onto the piazza from my window. It was still alive with voices, laughter, and the shuffle of feet on cobblestone.

Full Circle

Accursio spent my last day in Sciacca showing me more of the port. Just when I thought I had seen everything the marina had to offer, he revealed there was still more—tucked away and waiting to be discovered. Near the Porta di Mare, hidden between humble seafood shops, we came upon a set of subterranean caves. These ancient chambers, carved centuries ago by Carthaginian navigators, told a forgotten story.

Several of the caves connect through narrow passageways and were once used to store and protect wheat. Grain was poured in through a chute from above and later loaded onto caravels, rowboats, and whaling ships bound for the African coast. The ingenuity of it all astounded me—how deeply history was etched into every stone of this town.

Today, the Cultural Association of Sciacca is working to revitalize the caves. The site now hosts guided tours and artistic events, giving new life to this ancient, overlooked corner of the harbor.

After we toured the caves, Accursio insisted I eat something. The antibiotics had left me queasy, and I craved something light—preferably soup. But right next door was Bar Roma di Aurelio, and Accursio claimed they served the best *granita al limone* in all of Sicily. I followed him inside.

It was served on a *brioche*, a distinctly Italian twist—pairing icy citrus granita or creamy gelato with a soft, buttery

French bun. Though I usually went for chocolate or vanilla, I took his suggestion. As the tart ice melted into the pillowy bread, I was surprised at how much I liked it. Still, next time, I'd stick with *brioche con gelato*—the creamy version was more my style.

On the way back to my apartment, we spotted Cousin Santo driving toward the docks to pick up fresh fish for that evening's dinner—my last supper with the family. As we passed the cluster of small shops and restaurants, I noticed *La Bottega del Porto*. The gate was locked. I peeked through wistfully. At least now I knew exactly where it was. Next time.

Accursio had to leave for his night shift at the station, and I had plans for my final afternoon in Sciacca. I'd be catching the *autobus* to the airport at six in the morning. As we hugged goodbye, he surprised me—he said he'd be heading to Palermo, too, and would walk me to the station in the morning. "I'll be outside by five twenty," I promised.

Once he was gone, it hit me—I hadn't picked up my bus ticket yet. I walked toward the depot, smiling when I passed a fruit truck that looked just like the ones from my childhood in Brooklyn. Life in Sciacca felt so fresh, so human.

Usually, I avoided the main road—Giuseppe always seemed to pop up, scooter and all, like clockwork. Didn't he have a job? But this time, I had no choice. I had to cut through the park to reach the ticket counter. I debated stopping for one last order of calamari—my favorite treat—but hesitated, not wanting an audience.

No sign of Giuseppe. I took the chance.

The vendor grinned when he saw me. I'd become a regular.

"*Senza limone, sì?*" he asked knowingly.

I smiled and nodded. For once, I got to enjoy my crispy, golden morsels of squid and tentacles in peace, under the soft shadows of the trees. My last meal in Sciacca—and it was perfect.

I passed through the piazza on my way to dinner at Santo's. Hundreds of birds cut across the orange and purple sunset, their wings flashing in and out of the fading light. As they scrambled to nestle into the treetops for the night, their noisy chorus drowned out the usual hum of traffic and conversation. It felt like a farewell symphony.

I arrived at Santo's house with another decadent dessert in hand—my unofficial entry ticket. Giusy had prepared a *torta di patate*, a savory potato pie made with layers of *filo* dough, filled with potatoes, prosciutto, mozzarella, and oregano. She promised to send me the recipe.

"*Ti preparerò una pizza la prossima volta,*" Santo said, pointing proudly to his pizza oven. *I'll make you a pizza next time.* It was the second oven I'd seen built into someone's kitchen. In Sicily, a pizza oven seemed more essential than a microwave or even a dishwasher.

It made me think of backyard barbecues back in the States—how outdoor grills were often the man's territory. Maybe it was a similar thing here. Men took pride in their pizzas the way they did burgers and steaks at home. Only here, the pizza was art.

Santo asked when I'd return. "April," I said, and added—half-promise, half-confession—"I'll speak better Italian by then."

Dinner was delicious, as always. But when I took a bite of the swordfish, cut into thick circles instead of fillets, I got a mouthful of bones—*again*. They'd fooled me twice now.

It was still dark when I woke on my last morning in Sciacca. A quiet heaviness settled over me—I wasn't ready to leave.

There's something romantic about living in Sicily. Life moves slower. The air feels softer. Even the people seem more at ease with themselves and with time. All the reasons that once drove my grandfather away now made me want to stay.

The idea of moving here had become more than just a daydream. But as much as I loved the thought of planting roots in this old, familiar soil, I couldn't ignore the pull from the other side of the world. My life—messy, beautiful, unfinished—was still waiting for me.

As the saying goes, sometimes you can't go back home. But that doesn't make me any less Italian. Sicily is part of me. It's in my blood, in my memories, in the stories I carry forward.

And as long as there's sauce on Sunday, I will always be Sicilian.

Thank you for reading Sauce on Sunday. Please visit Amazon.com and post a helpful review.

Check out other Italian-based books by Janet Sierzant.

Asunder
Brooklyn Love Story
Gemini Joe
A Made Man

Recipes

Jeanette Corrao's Sunday Gravy

Start by sweating a half of an onion, finely chopped in two tablespoons of olive oil until they are transparent. This will sweeten the gravy. Add a healthy tablespoon of chopped garlic until browned. To prevent it from burning, I like to skim it out before browning any meat, such as sausage or pork.

Pulse two cans of whole canned tomatoes in a blender. My mother used to strain out the seeds over a strainer, but since the invention of the blended, seeds act as a thickening agent. Nowadays, people buy their tomato from a can. And why not, it's easier than having to boil down fresh whole tomatoes. Just make sure you get the highest quality brand to avoid a tinny taste. Season with salt, red pepper basil and oregano.

Meat – This is what makes it gravy. There are many kinds of meat that can be added, but it's essential to have at least two for the flavor. Typically, meatballs and some kind of pork product is best. My father always loved a leg of lamb. If you like this flavor instead of pork, make sure you brown it first and simmer in the sauce until it is fork tender…

Meatballs – For every pound of chopped meat add four eggs, half-cup seasoned breadcrumb, 1 tablespoon of minced garlic, quarter cup parmesan cheese, tsp salt, tsp black pepper, and a tablespoon of parsley. Wet hands and form into golf-size balls and fry in vegetable oil until all sides are brown. Gently place in sauce and simmer 3-4 hours.

Ricotta Pie

Filling	Crust
6 eggs	2 cups flour
1 cup of white sugar	2 ½ tsp baking powder
1 tsp vanilla	½ cup shortening, chill
24 ounces of ricotta cheese	½ cup of sugar
Chocolate chips	1 ½ tsp more shortening
	2 eggs, lightly beaten
	½ tsp vanilla

Filling: Beat eggs, sugar, and vanilla. Stir in ricotta and chips.

Crust: Combine flour, baking powder, and sugar. Cut in shortening until coarse and crumbly. Mix in eggs and vanilla. Divide into two balls, wrap, and chill for 30 minutes. Roll out the first ball and place it in a pie pan. Fill with ricotta mixture. Roll out the second ball. Cut into strips and crisscross on top of the pie, covering the edges with foil.

In a 350-degree oven, bake for 20 minutes, then remove foil. Rotate the pie in the oven and continue baking for another 20-25 minutes. Cool and chill.

Coponata

½ cup of balsamic
1 onion diced
5 tbsp. olive oil
2 cups diced eggplants
2 ½ cups diced zucchini
2 ½ cups diced yellow squash
3 sliced garlic cloves
Small can of diced tomatoes

2 ½ cups diced celery
½ cup diced red pepper
1 cup pitted Kalamata olives
2 tbsp. parsley
2 tbsp. oregano
Asiago cheese
Baguette

Boil the vinegar with the sugar over moderately high heat for about 5 minutes. Let cool. Heat some olive oil (3 tbsp..) in a non-stick skillet. Add the diced eggplant, 1-inch dice, season with salt and pepper, and cook over moderately high heat for 2 minutes, then reduce the heat to low and occasionally stir until the eggplant is tender. (About 10 minutes.) Transfer the eggplant to a large bowl. Wipe the skillet and heat the remaining olive oil. Add the zucchini and yellow squash, 1 inch diced, and cook until tender. Transfer to the bowl with the eggplant. Add the garlic, 1/2-inch diced celery, and onion to the skillet and cook over moderate heat until softened slightly. Add the bell pepper and cook until the vegetables are tender. Transfer to the bowl. Add drained and chopped tomatoes, olives, parsley, oregano, and balsamic syrup, and fold gently. Season with salt and pepper. Transfer to a clean bowl. Garnish with cheese. (Serve 4)

Pistachio Cream

3.5 ounces of unsalted, shelled pistachios
3 tbsp. of sugar
1 ounce of butter
1/2 cup of milk
1 tsp. of vanilla

Add your pistachios to a pot of boiling water and cook for a minute or so. Drain and remove the skins of each pistachio with your fingers or rub with a dry dish towel.

Heat oven to 350°F and roast pistachios on a baking sheet until lightly brown (for about 10 minutes). Remove from the oven and let cool. In a food processor, grind toasted pistachios with sugar. Add just enough milk to make the mixture creamy and smooth. Melt the rest of the milk and the butter in a small pot. (Do not boil!). Add in the pistachio mixture and the vanilla extract. Keep cooking on low heat for 6-8 minutes until it becomes dense. Remove from the heat, let cool, and pour into a clean jar. Refrigerate until you're ready to use it.

Creamy Salmon and Pasta

6 Tbsp. of butter
½ chopped onion
2 tbsp. of flour
2 tsp garlic powder
2 cups of milk
½ cup of Romano
1 cup of peas
½ cup mushrooms
10 ounces of Salmon sliced thin
Penne Pasta

Cook pasta for 8 to 10 minutes or until al dente; drain. Melt butter in a large skillet over medium heat. Sauté the onion in butter until tender. Stir flour and garlic powder into the butter and onions. Gradually stir in milk. Heat to below the boiling point, and gradually stir in the cheese until the sauce is smooth. Stir in peas and mushrooms and cook over low heat for four minutes. Toss in smoked salmon and cook for two more minutes. Serve over pasta. (Serves 4)

Eggplant and Sausage

1/4 cup balsamic vinegar
5 tbsp. extra-virgin olive oil
1 eggplant, cut ½ inch cubes
1 zucchini, sliced ½ inch cubes
1 yellow squash sliced ½ inch cubes
2 large celery ribs, chopped
2 garlic cloves, minced
1 onion, cut into 1/2-inch pieces
1 red bell pepper, sliced ½ inch cubes
1 green bell pepper, sliced ½ inch
1 lb. browned sausage
One can chop tomatoes
1 cup pitted kalamata olives
2 tbsp. parsley
2 tbsp. oregano
Shaved parmesan cheese

In a large nonstick skillet, heat olive oil until shimmering. Add the diced eggplant, zucchini, and yellow squash. Season with salt and pepper and cook until tender. Transfer to a bowl. Brown sausage with garlic, celery, and onion, and cook until slightly softened. Add peppers and cook until tender. Transfer to the eggplant and squash. Add the tomatoes, olives, parsley, oregano, and balsamic syrup, and fold gently. Season with salt and pepper. Garnish with the shaved Parmesan cheese.

Seafood Paella

1 large onion, finely chopped
5 tbsp. olive oil
2 garlic cloves, crushed to a paste or finely chopped
2 tomatoes, peeled and chopped
Salt
2 cups medium Arborio rice
3 cups fish or chicken stock, plus more if needed
1 cup dry white wine
Seafood Pack (shrimp, squid, mussels)

Saute the onion in the oil until soft in a pan with a heat-resistant handle to use in the oven. Brown the garlic, and add the tomatoes. Add salt to taste and paprika. Stir well, and cook until the tomatoes reduce. Add all fish except the shrimp, stirring, for a minute or so. Add the rice and stir well until all the grains are coated.

Bring the stock and wine to a boil in a saucepan. Pour over the rice, boil, and add salt to taste. Stir well and cover. Place in the pan in a 450°F oven for about twenty minutes. Lay the shrimp on top for 10 minutes until they turn pink. Add a little more hot stock toward the end if the rice seems too dry or a bit more cornstarch if too liquid.

Artichoke Hearts

6 whole artichokes
1 clove of garlic, chopped
4 tbsp. butter
2 eggs, beaten
1 tsp of parmesan cheese

Take off the leaves of the artichokes and pull out the hearts (minus the hairs). Chop them into bite-sized chunks. Brown garlic in butter, and then add the artichokes. Cook until tender. Add eggs and stir slightly. Season with salt, pepper, and sprinkle with cheese.

Boil artichoke leaves until tender, then season with salt, pepper, parmesan, and breadcrumbs. Drizzle with olive oil and bake until golden brown. (Serve 4-6)

Pasticcotti Pockets

Custard Filling
3 tbsp. cornstarch
1/2 cup sugar
1/2 cup heavy cream
1 cup milk
2 egg yolks
1 tbsp. butter
1 tsp. almond extract
1 egg, beaten
Pastry crust

Place sifted cornstarch and sugar in a saucepan. Add milk and cream, then whisk lightly until smooth. Add a beaten egg and heat until the custard gets thick. Add butter and almond extract. Remove and place a piece of plastic wrap over the container.

Roll out pastry dough on a floured board, 1/4" thick. Cut rounds using a 3" glass. Add about 2 tbsp. Of the custard to each side and cover with a second layer. Run a fork around the edges to seal the crust and chill in the refrigerator for an hour or overnight. Brush tops with egg wash, then bake at 425°F for 15 minutes.

Zucchini Pesto

2 small, grated zucchinis
1 clove garlic
2 tbsp. ground pistachio nuts
1/2 cup grated Parmesan cheese
1/4 cup fresh basil leaves
salt & pepper to taste
2-4 tbsp. extra virgin olive oil
1-pound dried pasta

Thoroughly squeeze all excess water from the grated zucchini with a dishtowel. Place zucchini in a food processor with garlic, pine nuts, parmesan, basil, and salt & pepper. With the food processor running, drizzle in the olive oil until the pesto reaches the consistency you like. Check for seasoning again and adjust as necessary. Bring a pot of water to a boil and cook pasta according to package directions. Drain pasta and toss with pesto to thoroughly coat.

Sausage with Lemon and Oregano

3 cloves of garlic
1/4 cup fresh oregano
1/2 cup extra virgin olive oil
Juice of 2 lemons
Salt & pepper to taste

Brown whole coil sausage in a little olive oil. While cooking, grind garlic and mix it with oregano, olive oil, and lemon juice. Toss the lemon skins into the pan with the sausage. Once the sausage cooks, pour the oregano and lemon mixture over and simmer for one minute. Transfer to a dish and arrange lemon slices as garnish. (Serves 4)

Pistachio Pesto

Fresh basil leaves
2 cups shelled pistachios
1/2 parmesan cheese
2 cloves of garlic
½ cup of olive oil
Salt and pepper to taste

Pulse the dry ingredients together in a blender until finely chopped. Drizzle in the olive oil while blending slowly until smooth. Mix with pasta or mashed potatoes.

Stuffed Squid in Tomato Sauce

8-10 whole squid bodies
2 cups of breadcrumbs
½ minced onion
4 cloves of minced garlic
½ cup of Romano or Parmesan cheese
2 tbsp. of parsley
2 eggs
Optional - chopped shrimp
¼ cup olive oil
1 can of whole tomatoes (blended to puree)
1 pound of any Pasta

Combine breadcrumbs, onion, garlic, cheese, parsley, and eggs to make the stuffing. Shrimp or crabmeat could be used if desired, but not necessary. Stuff the squid bodies, secure them with toothpicks, and brown them in olive oil.

Cook pasta for 8 to 10 minutes or until it puffs up. Add tomato sauce and cover. Simmer low for at least one hour. Al dente; drain. Serve squid over pasta. (Serves 4)

Anisette Cookies

3-4 cups flour
3 ½ tsp baking powder
1 cup of sugar
½ tsp salt
6 eggs
¼ bottle of anise
½ cup of vegetable oil
Lemon extract
Confection sugar

Mix flour, baking powder, sugar, and salt. Add eggs, anise, and oil, and gently fold to mix. Divide the dough into equal small parts. Take each piece and roll it on the counter into long worms. Cut into four-inch sections and coil them to make the cookie. Bake at 350 degrees. Glaze with lemon mixture. (Confection sugar, water, and lemon extract combined to a silky consistency)

Giusy's Potato Pie

Italian
1 bollire le patate (mezzo chilo).
2 condire le patate con (sale origano tonno) amalgamare tutto
3 mettere la pasta sfoglia (rotonda) in una teglia
4 mettere il condimento con le patate sulla pasta sfoglia
5 infornare a 180 per 40 minuti
6 dopo 40 minuti uscire la torta e aggiungere un po' di mozzarella, il tempo che la mozzarella si scioglie, la torta può essere sfornata

English
1. Boil the potatoes (half a kilo).
2. Season the potatoes with oregano and tuna. and mix everything
3. Put the puff pastry (round) in a pan
4. Put the dressing with the potatoes on the puff pastry
5. Bake at 180 °C for 40 minutes

6 Take out after 40 minutes and add a little mozzarella. The time that the mozzarella melts, the cake can be baked.

Giusy Ruffo

Giuseppe and Anna Corrao

Corrao daughters - Left to right.
Anna Lucy, Mary, Jeanette, Phyllis

Corrao Sisters

Riley was happy to see me when I got home, but every time I left the apartment, I'd see him looking at me from the window. He was probably wondering if I was coming back or leaving him again. It took a while for him to let me out of his sight, but he's doing fine.

They say that dogs are man's best friend
But I do disagree
Felines are the species best
and very dear to me
Independent, yes, it's true
But loving when at rest
He plops down in my bed at night
And puts it to the test
With the sun
he waits for me
to rise and say hello
He flips his tail and meows for food
his hunger, he does show
His stomach full, I have less fear
That he will eat a mouse
I let him out, but he returns
with gifts into the house

Look for other books by Janet Sierzant
Asunder – Italian Historical Fiction
Brooklyn Love Story – Fiction Romance
Gemini Joe – Memoirs of Brooklyn
The Green Room – A Psychological Fiction

Coming Soon
A Made Man – A Mafia Fiction

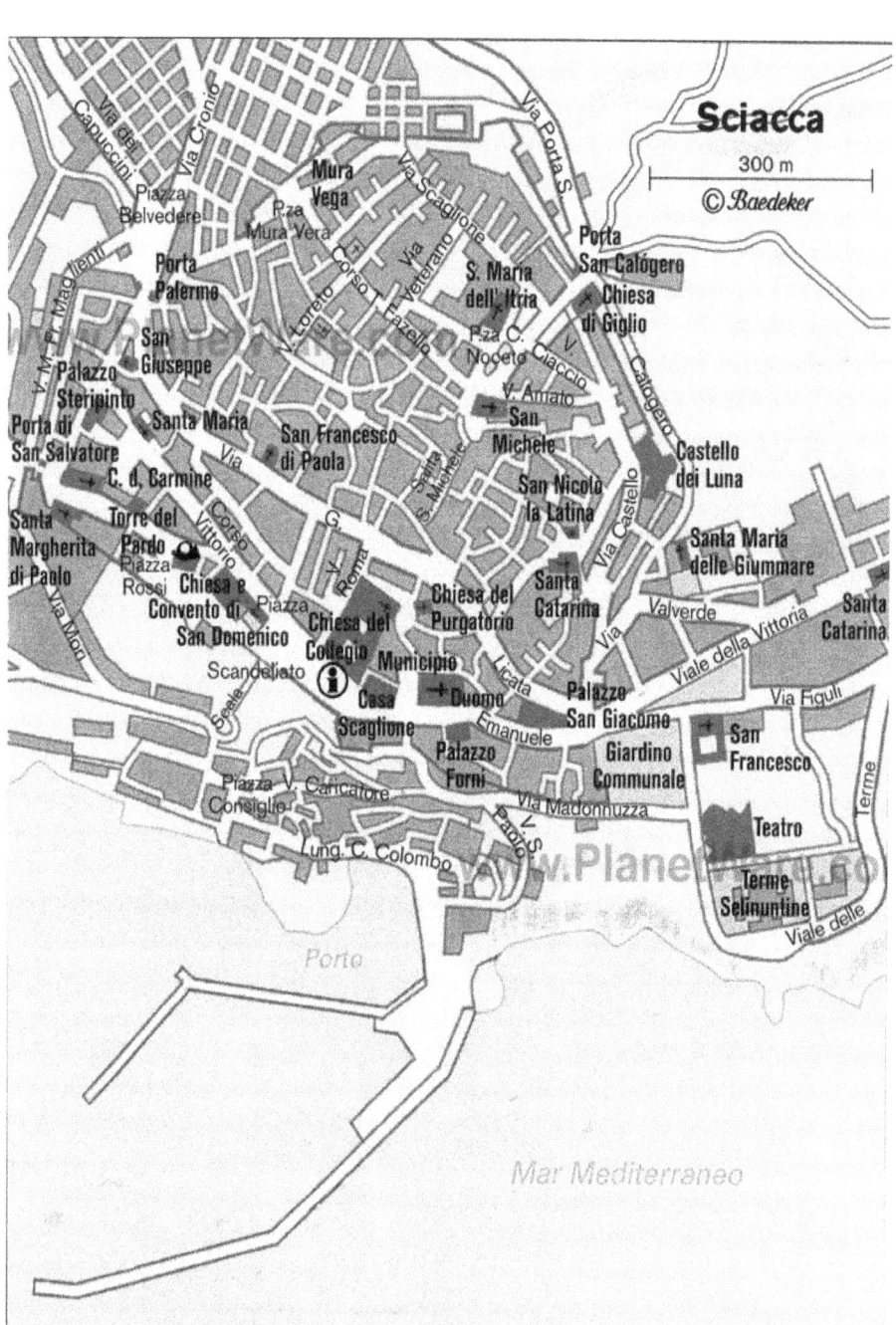

www.ingramcontent.com/pod-product-compliance
Lightning Source LLC
Chambersburg PA
CBHW042131160426
43199CB00021B/2876